# 100 GREAT GUITARISTS

## And the Gear That Made Them Famous

by Dave Rubin

T0057724

To access audio visit:
**www.halleonard.com/mylibrary**

Enter Code
1566-9763-7556-8984

ISBN 978-1-5400-0303-4

7777 W. BLUEMOUND RD. P.O. BOX 13819 MILWAUKEE, WI 53213

In Australia Contact:
**Hal Leonard Australia Pty. Ltd.**
4 Lentara Court
Cheltenham, Victoria, 3192 Australia
Email: ausadmin@halleonard.com.au

Visit Hal Leonard Online at
**www.halleonard.com**

# CONTENTS

Recorded, mixed, and mastered by Doug Boduch

# Acknowledgments and Dedication

Thanks to Jeff Schroedl, Kurt Plahna, and everyone at Hal Leonard for their invaluable help and encouragement on this project. I would like to dedicate this book to Anthony Mixon, Jim Schustedt, and Gus Smalley.

# Guitar Gear: From the Bow to the EBow and Beyond

It is likely that the first stringed instrument and primary ancestor of the guitar was a bow, originally used to propel an arrow, after it was discovered that it could make a pleasing sound when plucked. An early example in the evolution of the concept comes from Mesopotamia c. 4500 B.C., as evidence of "bow harps" with long necks and small rectangular bodies were found in the region. In Sumeria around 2600 B.C., there existed the *pantur*, that literally means "small bow," and is also believed to be another term for lute. "Bowl harps," instruments with curved necks and bowl-shaped bodies made from tortoise shells and calabashes, existed in Sumerian, Babylonian, and Egyptian cultures as early as 2000 B.C. Most significantly, the latter civilization also had the *tanbur*, with a long, straight neck that allowed the string to be pressed to the neck for additional pitches. It was connected to a small, egg-shaped body with an arched back and a soundboard made from hide or wood. Around 1300 B.C., the Turks pictured in bas-relief a startling guitar-like instrument with curved sides and what look like frets.

Many other cultures also had their own idiosyncratic variations. These include the Hebrew *kinura* (kinnor), the Assyrian *chetarah*, and the Greek *lyra* and *cithara*, which was later adopted by the Romans. The long-necked Greek *pandura*, as pictured in 400 B.C., is similar to the Egyptian tanbur and is the forerunner of the various families of lutes, as well as the bouzouki. The pandura had three strings and is cited as the first instrument to have frets.

By the seventh century in Persia, the *setar* existed with twenty-five to twenty-six moveable catgut frets and three strings (with a fourth added much later in the mid-eighteenth century). It was a direct descendant of the pear-shaped, two-string tanbur that had been in use for two hundred years and would eventually influence the design of the Indian sitar. In the eighth century, the conquering Moors brought to Spain the fretless, four-string *al'ud* ("the wood") or *oud* that may have originated in Mecca c. 685, and by 1200 had developed into the pear-shaped *guitarra morisca* (Moorish guitar). It is worth noting that "guit" is the Arab word for "four" and "tar" the word for "string." Concurrent with the guitarra morisca was the *guitarra latina* with four courses of strings and curved sides; this was likewise being played in Spain, though it probably arrived from Europe rather than Persia.

The oud would precede the lute (a transliteration of 'ud)—that ubiquitous European symbol of troubadours in the medieval era—which has a bowl for the body, a headstock bent back at a ninety-degree angle, six to ten courses, or pairs, of "catgut" (sheep intestine) strings, and moveable catgut frets that were tied on. Numerous paintings and prints of lute players exist from the fifteenth and sixteenth centuries.

However, it is the *cittern,* which existed around the same time, that is considered the first true guitar. Apparently originating in Italy but extensively developed in England, it is a flat-backed instrument with four or five courses of metal strings and a straight headstock, as shown in the famous painting "The Guitar Player" (c. 1672) by Dutch master Jan Vermeer, as well as in four of his other works. Additionally, in 1677, the Dutch artist Pieter van Slingeland painted "Woman with Cittern." Most significantly, the cittern had fixed brass frets and was plucked with a crow quill. As opposed to the polite society lute, the cittern was shunned as a low-class instrument popular in taverns, barber shops, and bordellos where its superior volume was well-served. The name itself would become a slang term for promiscuous women, perhaps leading to the words "slattern" and "slut."

The Renaissance era and thereafter produced a huge number of variations on the design of stringed instruments across Europe. Meanwhile, the lute continued to reign over the guitar in popularity, except in Spain due to its resented connection to the conquering Moors. Many other instruments with courses of strings and moveable frets followed, including the German *fiedel,* the French *vielle,* and the Spanish *guitarra* and *vihuela.* The latter has six courses of strings tuned similarly to today's standard tuning, was plucked with the fingers, and was a major step along the way toward the modern guitar.

The Baroque guitar, known for its rich ornamentation, five courses, and fixed frets, was developed in the early 1700s. By the middle of the century, six-string guitars with permanent frets were being prominently made in Italy and Germany and were also showing up c. 1820 in Spain as their popularity spread to become the norm. Small parlor guitars with gut strings also began appearing at this time while the classical guitar would be further developed after 1840 in Spain by luthier Antonio de Torres. In 1833, luthier Christian Friedrich "C.F." Martin emigrated from Germany to the U.S. and set up shop in downtown Manhattan where he began building high-quality guitars. He was not the first guitar maker in America; there was one in colonial Williamsburg and other areas. Nonetheless, Martin would go on to become the premier acoustic flat-top guitar producer, even as others like the Lyon and Healy company outsold him in the late 1800s with their cheaper Washburn brand, including the popular 1887 model.

In various guises, like the ponderous harp guitars made by Gibson around the turn of the twentieth century and their revolutionary L-5 archtop with f-holes in 1922, wooden acoustic guitars strung mainly with steel strings would be common until the twenties. But the desire to create a louder instrument that could compete in an ensemble setting with brass and drums finally reached fruition in 1926 with the National Steel resonator guitar, and in 1928 with the Dobro. Concurrently, attempts were being made to build a practical amplified or electric guitar. In 1932, Adolph Rickenbacher, in conjunction with George Beauchamp (who had worked for National), introduced one of the first solidbody electric guitars, known as the "frying pan" due to its shape. Lloyd Loar, who had been employed by Gibson and designed the famous L-5, started the Vivi-Tone company in the early thirties that produced a number of hollow electric guitars and accompanying amps. Likewise, Dobro also began making electrics during this decade. In 1936, however, Gibson trumped everyone by introducing the first commercially-successful electric guitar with their ES-150 archtop and matching 15-watt EH-150 amplifier. A musical revolution would ensue, helped in large part by jazz guitarist Charlie Christian's embrace of the exciting, new instrument in Benny Goodman's swing band, and then by his counterpart, blues guitar legend T-Bone Walker, who favored the fancier ES-250.

Inventor Paul Bigsby began building solidbody guitars in the forties, including one for Merle Travis in 1948 that has surprising features later found on Fenders and Gibsons. Meanwhile, both Les Paul and Leo Fender were also experimenting with solidbody electric guitar designs. Paul had tried to sell Gibson on the idea in the early forties after building and performing with his "log," which consisted of a 4x4 chunk of lumber with acoustic guitar "wings" added for looks; he was turned down as his creation was derided as a "broomstick with pickups." But working independently in California, Leo Fender had a radical solidbody ready to play by 1950. First called the Broadcaster, it was mated to the small amps he had been producing since 1945 to go with his lap steels, and the combination would soon find great favor with the country bands that Fender so admired.

In 1952, Gibson finally came around to the idea of a solidbody electric guitar (with the input of Paul) after being lapped by Fender. The Les Paul Goldtop was a much different instrument than the Broadcaster/Esquire/Telecaster in design, sound, and most significantly, its superior sustain, which would come to define the sound of the electric guitar in rock from the late sixties onward. Although Gibson had been making quality amps since the late thirties, Fender would soon surpass them in power, reliability, and innovations such as tremolo and reverb. Ironically, with serious competition only from Ampeg in the late fifties, Fender would prove to be a perfect conduit for Gibson and virtually all other guitars.

Fender, Gibson, and their main competitors, Epiphone, Gretsch, Guild, and Rickenbacker, made great, classic instruments during the "golden age" in the fifties as rock 'n' roll, not coincidentally, developed at the same time. However, it would take the Beatles and the Rolling Stones-led British Invasion in the mid sixties, and the counterculture explosion that followed, to push the sonic envelope considerably further for the electric guitar. In the talented hands of Jeff Beck of the Yardbirds, heavy fuzz box distortion and feedback became expressive improvisational tools when combined with Vox AC30 amps, which the Beatles likewise utilized for admittedly less-extreme results. Pushing dynamic volume and feedback to the maximum as a compositional element, the Who contributed to the development of Marshall amps (originally patterned on the Fender Bassman), which would bring out the beast in the Les Paul and Fender Strat. In the U.S., Jimi Hendrix became the uncontested wizard of new effects, ganging the wah-wah pedal, phase shifter, octave box, and fuzz box together in conjunction with the whammy bar on his Strat to create magical, otherworldly sounds.

By the seventies, the envelope follower, flanger, analog delay, and a dizzying array of distortion boxes were an accepted and expected part of the sonic palette of the hip, electric guitarist. Unusual and eccentric effects appeared as well, like the "talk box" and the EBow; the former was featured on a handful of hit recordings such as "Rocky Mountain Way" (Joe Walsh) and "Do You Feel Like We Do" (Peter Frampton), but ultimately proved to be a gimmick. The latter, however, was an intelligent attempt at producing infinite natural sustain by hovering the hand-held device over the desired string, creating an electromagnetic field that could keep the string vibrating indefinitely for a stunning legato effect. Unfortunately, it would prove unwieldy for most guitarists and an impediment to conventional techniques such as string bending and damping. But the race was on for sustain, resulting in preamps and master volume controls on amps for more controlled overdrive, more powerful replacement humbucking and single-coil pickups, heavier brass hardware on guitars for greater mass, and unconventional body materials such as Lucite, aluminum, and even stone! Later on, graphite and composites were also tried, all of which contributed to increasing natural sustain. One of the most practical and lasting solutions for massive sustain was the Power Soak, invented and used by Tom Scholz of Boston fame. Operating from the theory that the most natural overdriven amp tone and sustain comes from cranked power tubes rather than preamp tubes, he devised a way to play even Marshall stacks on "10," with the overall volume adjustable down to acceptable levels.

The eighties witnessed new wave bands strip down their sound to clean, jangly guitars with chorusing added for color and digital delay added for ambience; metal bands went in the opposite direction with racks of separate solid-state components including preamps, various reverbs, delays, graphic equalizers, and compressors, among other tone modifiers. Small guitar makers sprang up and produced aggressive, non-traditional shapes to service the "hair bands," including Charvel, Jackson, Kramer, and Dean. High-output pickups for extreme overdrive were all the rage and often combined with locking nuts and roller bridges to facilitate vigorous whammy bar action without breaking strings or going out of tune.

One of the most significant advances in amp design into the new millennium was modeling amps capable of faithfully and digitally imitating a wide variety of classic amp and speaker combinations from the past. And, in "what is old is new," the trend toward small, boutique tube amps, capable of being miked through large PA systems if necessary, blossomed in the nineties and continues today. At the same time and in the same vein, Fender has maintained a steady reissue program of their classic, "low-tech" tube amp combos from the fifties and sixties.

Dave Rubin

# DUANE ALLMAN

© Amalie R. Rothschild

Ever the rebel, **Howard Duane Allman** (1946–1971) was once asked what he was doing for peace and replied, "Eat a peach." A supremely talented and confident musician, Duane brought the older blues technique of bottleneck guitar to the fore in the late sixties. He was dubbed "Sky Dog" by the R&B cats with whom he played before he assembled his "dream team" in 1969 with his brother Gregg, guitarist Dickey Betts, bassist Berry Oakley, and drummers Butch Trucks and Johnny Lee "Jaimoe" Johanson. He completed work on *The Allman Brothers Band, Idlewild South, Live at Fillmore East*, as well as contributed to *Eat a Peach* before he tragically died in a motorcycle accident. Allman was inducted into the Rock and Roll Hall of Fame with the Allman Brothers Band (ABB) in 1986.

## The Sound

Allman distinguished his playing through natural tube distortion with a biting, trebly edge. Purportedly, Allman played a dot-neck Gibson ES-335 through a black-face Fender Twin Reverb on the first ABB album; the 335 was superseded by a 1957 Les Paul Goldtop and eventually traded to Dickey Betts for a 1961 SG. Next came a 1958 "cherry burst" Les Paul Standard and his famous 1959 "tobacco burst" Les Paul Standard that he fried through Marshall heads and cabinets.

**Guitar:** 1959 Gibson Les Paul Standard
**Amp:** 50-watt Marshall head with Marshall 100 bass cabinet

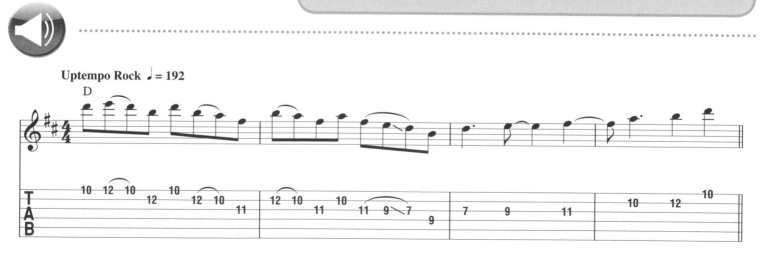

# TREY ANASTASIO

A college education in the early eighties contributed to **Ernesto Joseph "Trey" Anastasio III** (1964– ) gaining advanced musical concepts beyond that of the era's average rock guitarist. After forming Phish at the University of Vermont in 1983 with songwriting partner Tom Marshall, drummer Jon Fishman, bassist Mike Gordon, and guitarist Jeff Holdsworth, Anastasio would go on to lead the band through progressive compositions featuring atonal music starting with *Junta* in 1988. Eventually, the music evolved into long, improvisational jams, spearheading the jam band movement, until the band's dissolution in 2000. Concurrently and down to the present, Anastasio has convened and played in a number of ambitious projects. In 2002, he released his first, self-titled solo outing, and in 2009, he completed *Time Turns Elastic* with guitarist Don Hart.

## The Sound

Besides being a "neo-deadhead," Anastasio is a ravenous gear head who uninhibitedly explores his music with a thick, rich palette of swirling, processed tones. Recently his setup included a Paul Languedoc Custom Thinline electric archtop and a Martin DCE Trey Anastasio Signature flat-top, along with a Fender Deluxe Reverb, Mesa Boogie Mark III head, Bruno 4x12 speaker cabinet, Languedoc 2x12 speaker cabinets, and a Leslie 122 speaker cabinet.

© Sony/BMG

**Guitar:** Paul Languedoc Custom thinline electric archtop

**Amp:** Fender Deluxe Reverb and Mesa Boogie Mark III

**Effects:** Furman Power Conditioner, Ibanez DM-2000 Delay and Tube Screamers (with Analog Man TS9/808 Silver Mod), Custom Audio Electronics 4x4 Switcher, Super Tremolo, Black Cat Vibe, RS-10 MIDI Foot Controller and ISO-1, Alesis Microverb I and Nanoverbs, Dunlop GCB-95 wah pedal, Boss FS-5L Leslie and FS-5U, Ernie Ball volume pedal, DigiTech Whammy II, Boomerang Phrase Sampler, CAE Super Tremolo, Trek II UC-1A Leslie pre-amp

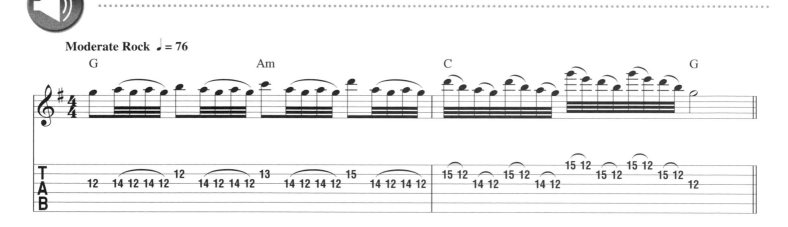

Moderate Rock ♩ = 76

# CHET ATKINS

The legendary **Chester Burton Atkins** (1924–2001) clearly earned the sobriquet, "Mr. Guitar." Influenced by everyone from Mother Maybelle Carter to Django Reinhardt and especially Merle Travis, Chet was a session guitarist for RCA in Nashville by 1949 and joined the Carter Sisters as a regular guitarist at the Grand Ole Opry in 1950. From 1953 through to the eighties, he produced and backed others for RCA while recording his own material, starting with his signature song, "Country Gentleman," which would eventually become the name of his signature Gretsch guitar. He jumped to Columbia Records in 1982 and began referring to himself as "Chet Atkins, C.G.P." The "Certified Guitar Player" would eventually net 14 Grammy Awards and nine Country Music Association Awards for Musician of the Year.

## The Sound

Atkins always favored a warm, acoustic-electric sound, starting in 1947 with a Gibson L-7 archtop with a DeArmond pickup through an early Fender Deluxe amp, followed by a D'Angelico Excel cutaway in the early fifties. In 1954 he sported a Gretsch 6120, and by 1958 he was playing a Gretsch Tennessean and his Gretsch County Gentleman guitar, followed by a Gretsch Super Chet, Chet Atkins Super Axe, and a Gibson Chet Atkins CE (classical electric) guitar.

© Pictorial Press Ltd. / Alamy

**Guitar:** 1954 Gretsch 6120, 1958 Gretsch Country Gentleman, mid-sixties Gretsch Nashville

**Amp:** Ray Butts EchoSonic, Standel 25L15

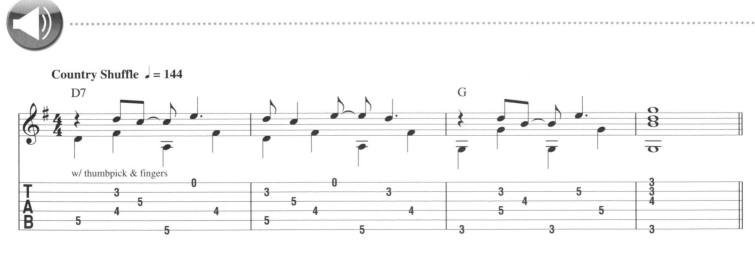

Country Shuffle ♩ = 144

w/ thumbpick & fingers

# JEFF BECK

British guitar god **Geoffrey Arnold "Jeff" Beck** (1944– ) is perhaps second only to Jimi Hendrix as a rock guitar innovator. In fact, he influenced Hendrix with his pioneering use of distortion and feedback while in the Yardbirds (1965–66). Before leaving the Yardbirds to go solo, Beck and Jimmy Page created a guitar freak's dream team in the band, after which "Pagey" would form Led Zeppelin. Starting with *Blow by Blow* in 1975, Beck has produced an unmatched catalog of melodic and blues-tinged instrumental rock albums featuring fingerpicking and his uniquely expressive use of the tremolo bar. In 1992, he was inducted into the Rock and Roll Hall of Fame as a member of the Yardbirds and in 2009 as a solo artist.

## The Sound

A bluesman at heart, Beck has favored a natural tube amp sound, even when using stomp boxes and extreme distortion. He played a utilitarian 1956 Fender Esquire through a Vox AC30 in the Yardbirds before graduating to a 1954 Les Paul Goldtop painted oxblood brown and fitted with humbuckers in place of the original P-90 pickups. Ultimately he turned to a Fender Strat through a Marshall amp during his solo career.

© Marty Temme

**Guitar:** 1956 Fender Esquire, 1954 Gibson Les Paul, **Fender Stratocaster**

**Amp:** Marshall JCM 2000, DSL50

**Effects:** Hughes & Kettner Rotosphere, Boss LS-2 line selectors, Boss BF-2 flanger, Maestro ring modulator, EBS Octabass

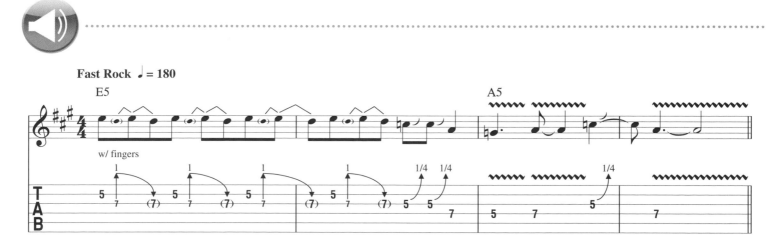

11

# GEORGE BENSON

© Fernando Aceves / Retna Ltd.

The musical heir of Wes Montgomery and Charlie Christian, **George Benson** (1943– ) built his reputation on the enticing combination of jazz and R&B. He made his singing debut as a four-year-old in Pittsburgh and by the age of ten was inked to a short-term contract with RCA in New York. He released the landmark *The New Boss Guitar of George Benson with The Brother Jack McDuff Quartet* in 1964, and in 1968 signed with A&M where his idol, Wes Montgomery, held forth. His spectacular breakthrough occurred in 1976 on Warner Bros. Records with the platinum-selling, Grammy-winning *Breezin'*, containing the monster pop vocal hit, "This Masquerade." The combination of his soulful singing and versatile, exceptional guitar work has continued to serve Benson well in his ongoing career.

## The Sound

As befits a guitarist raised on classic jazz, Benson has opted to play a variety of fine archtops over the years, including a Gibson Super 400, L5CES, and L5C, and a D'Angelico New Yorker. Since 1978, he has used Ibanez George Benson Signature guitars. Prior to *Breezin'*, he played Fender Twin Reverb amps before switching to the Polytone 104, a Polytone Mini-Brute V, and currently, Fender Hot Rod DeVille amps.

**Guitar:** Ibanez **GB10** and GB200
**Amp:** Fender Hot Rod DeVille

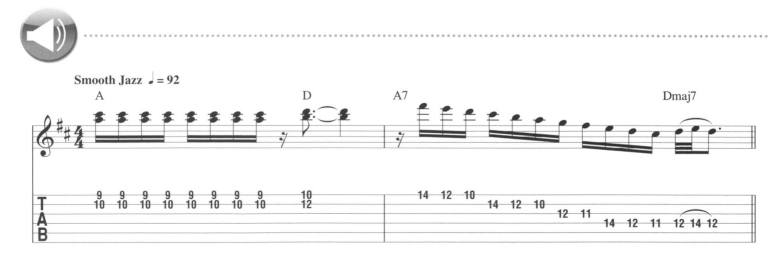

# CHUCK BERRY

**Charles Edward Anderson "Chuck" Berry** (1926–2017 ) was the undisputed "Father of Rock 'n' Roll." In East St. Louis in the forties, he developed a following by combining the blues, Nat King Cole, and country music in a manner that was unusual for a black artist. In 1954, he went to Chicago with a demo tape where Muddy Waters famously told him to, "Go see Leonard (Chess)" at Chess Records; subsequently, "Maybellene" produced a paradigm shift in rock 'n' roll history in 1955. Through to 1959 and then into the mid sixties, Berry wrote the "book" with "Roll Over, Beethoven," "Rock and Roll Music," "Johnny B. Goode," "Sweet Little Sixteen," "Nadine," and two dozen other classics. His vast influence on rock guitarists and the songwriting of the Beatles and Rolling Stones is incalculable.

## The Sound

Similar to B.B. King, Berry went through different bell ringers including an Epiphone Century, a 1952–53 Gibson ES-295, and a circa-1954 black Les Paul. Many of his most famous recordings from 1955 through to 1958, including "Johnny B. Goode," were made on a 1955 Gibson ES-350TN through tweed Fender amps. From around "Little Queenie" in late 1958 on, however, Berry played a succession of Gibson ES-355 guitars through Fender Dual Showman amps.

© Photofest

**Guitar:** 1955 Gibson ES-350TN

**Amp:** Tweed Fender Bassman, Fender Dual Showman

# NUNO BETTENCOURT

**Nuno Duarte Gil Mendes Bettencourt** (1966– ) was born in the Azores but moved to Boston as a child. His musical influences were Van Halen, the Beatles, Prince, and Queen, and he was a string-skipping electric guitar virtuoso by the time he joined Extreme in 1985. After three more albums, following their self-titled debut in 1989, the band split in 1996, and Bettencourt initiated a solo career. In 1997, he played all the instruments on *Schizophonic*, an album that veered away from the restrictive sound of Extreme. He recorded *Inspiration New York* in 2005 and the soundtrack for *Smart People* in 2008. In 2007, Extreme reunited to record *Saudades de Rock*, which was released in 2008. In 2009, Bettencourt began backing Rihanna while continuing his renewed relationship with Extreme.

## The Sound

Bettencourt prefers a saturated and effect-laden heavy metal tone. In 1990, Washburn introduced the Nuno Bettencourt Signature Series of Strat-type guitars that he designed. He has played a Hughes & Kettner TriAmp head with a seventies Marshall slant-front cabinet and currently is using Randall amps and cabinets, as well as Marshall and Fender amps.

© Robert Knight

**Guitar:** **Washburn N4 Nuno Bettencourt Signature solidbody electric,** Washburn N8 6/12 electric and EA-10 acoustic

**Amp:** Signature Randall NB King 100 head with Randall NB 412 cabinets

**Effects:** Boss ME-5 Multi Effects, Boss LS-2 Line Selector, Boss PS-3 Pitch Shifter/Delay, Boss OC-3 Octave, MXR Phase 100, Heil Talkbox, Hughes & Kettner Rotosphere, Damage Control Womanizer Pure Class A Distortion, ProCo Rat

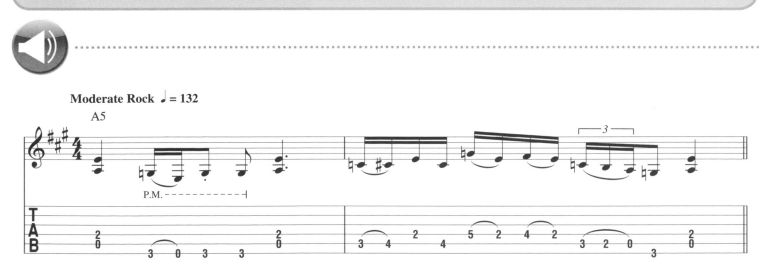

Moderate Rock ♩ = 132

# DICKEY BETTS

© Marty Temme

He was considered the "second guitarist" in the Allman Brothers Band; however, Floridian **Forrest Richard "Dickey" Betts** (1943– ) was the advanced guitarist in many ways, contributing songs, melodic solos, and sweet harmonic guitar lines with Duane on *Allman Brothers Band*, *Idlewild South*, *Live at Fillmore East*, and *Eat a Peach*. He assumed co-leader duties after Duane's death; this returned an immediate dividend when *Brothers and Sisters* was released in 1973, spotlighting his singing and playing. By the mid seventies, breakups and reunions would occur until Betts was unceremoniously asked to leave in 2000 (despite being inducted into the Rock and Roll Hall of Fame with the band in 1996). In 2001, he released the ironically-titled solo album, *Let's Get Together* and a live Dickey Betts & Great Southern album in 2008.

## The Sound

The classic, sustained Les Paul sound and Betts are synonymous. However, he originally played a Gibson ES-345 and a 1961 SG that he later traded to Duane for "Goldie," his iconic Gibson Les Paul Goldtop. In the ABB, he soared on Marshall amps with a cleaner blues tone than Duane. Gibson released Artist Authentic models in 2000 and 2002, but in later years, Betts became a Paul Reed Smith endorser.

**Guitar:** 1957 Gibson Les Paul Goldtop
**Amp:** Marshall 100-watt stack with JBL speakers

Fast Rock ♩ = 184

# RITCHIE BLACKMORE

© Marty Temme

In 1967, keyboardist Jon Lord invited former session guitarist **Richard Hugh Blackmore** (1945– ) to join the English Roundabout. As Deep Purple, in 1968, they cut *Shades of Deep Purple*. Following *Concerto for Group and Orchestra*, however, Blackmore took command and pushed his guitar to the fore. Loud proto-heavy metal ensued with *Deep Purple in Rock* (1970), *Fireball* (1971), *Machine Head* (containing "Smoke on the Water"), and *Live in Japan* (1972) to put the "Purps" in the company of Black Sabbath and Led Zeppelin, thanks to Blackmore's blazing speed and classically-influenced licks. In 1975, he left to form Rainbow with vocalist Ronnie James Dio. Various reunions would occur over the following decades. Since 1997, Blackmore has performed in the Renaissance-based Blackmore's Night with his wife, Candice Night.

## The Sound

Blackmore became a Strat man after seeing Jimi Hendrix, and he purchased one with a Telecaster neck that had belonged to Eric Clapton. From the seventies up to Blackmore's Night, he played post-CBS models which were given scalloped fingerboards and contributed to his signature, fluid microbends. He originally favored deafening Marshall Major 200-watt amps modified to 278 walls (!) until 1994, when he began using Engl tube amps and started to move away from guitar synthesizers.

**Guitar: Seventies Fender Stratocaster** and recent Fender Ritchie Blackmore Signature Stratocaster

**Amp:** Engl Ritchie Blackmore Signature 100

**Effects:** Hornby Skewes treble booster, EMS Synthi Hi-Fli guitar synthesizer, Moog Taurus bass pedals, Unicord Univibe, Dallas Arbiter Fuzz Face and Octave Divider.

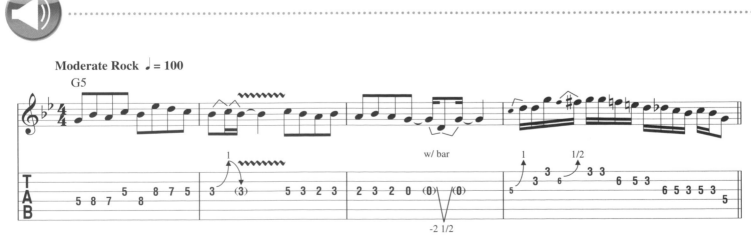

# MICHAEL BLOOMFIELD

**Michael Bernard Bloomfield** (1943–1981) was an authentic interpreter of the blues and one of the first modern American guitar heroes. He practiced in his suburban Chicago bedroom before realizing that the blues was being played live in downtown Chicago. In 1965, he joined Paul Butterfield and Elvin Bishop, along with a black rhythm section of Jerome Arnold and Sam Lay. Their debut, *Paul Butterfield Blues Band*, was followed by *East-West* in 1967 with its revolutionary modal fusion jams. However, he quit the band and formed the Electric Flag, KGB, and Triumvirate (the latter with John Hammond, Jr. and Dr. John), and even played on soundtracks for porn films. Tragically, in 1981, he overdosed on heroin and was found dead in his car on a street in San Francisco.

## The Sound

Bloomfield, the true bluesman, played a 1964 rosewood fingerboard Fender Telecaster, later traded for a 1956 Les Paul Goldtop with P-90 single-coil pickups, which he played through a 1963 Guild Thunderbird amp prototype on the first Butterfield album. After hearing Eric Clapton with a 1960 burst, he traded his Goldtop for a vintage '59 model. In the Electric Flag he played Fender Twins and Super Reverbs, always dedicated to unfiltered, natural, tube amp distortion.

© Photofest

**Guitar:** 1959 sunburst Gibson Les Paul Standard
**Amp:** Pre-CBS Fender Twin Reverb

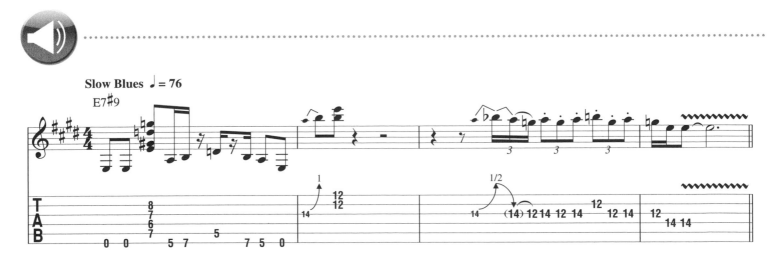

# BIG BILL BROONZY

Along with Memphis Minnie and Tampa Red, **William Lee Conley "Big Bill" Broonzy** (1903–1958) was one of the most influential pre-war acoustic guitarists in Chicago. He was also a prolific composer ("Key to the Highway"), as well as a top session cat in the twenties and thirties. In 1938, he performed at the landmark "From Spirituals to Swing" concert at Carnegie Hall in New York City in place of the recently-deceased Robert Johnson. Broonzy began experimenting with the electric guitar in 1945, but by the 1950s he had turned to a folkier style of acoustic music and toured Europe. His fame was such in England that George Harrison sang the lyrics, "Feel Like Big Bill Broonzy," on "Wreck of the Hesperus" from *Cloud 9* (1987).

## The Sound

Photographic evidence shows Broonzy with a Regal flat-top, c. 1920 Gibson Style O "Artist" mandolin scroll archtop and a Bacon and Day Senorita in the twenties and thirties. In the forties, he played a National electric with an accompanying amp, Epiphone Deluxe, and a Gibson L-7. In the fifties, he played a Martin 000-28.

**Guitar:** Early-twenties Gibson
Style O Artist archtop acoustic

© Pictorial Press Ltd / Alamy

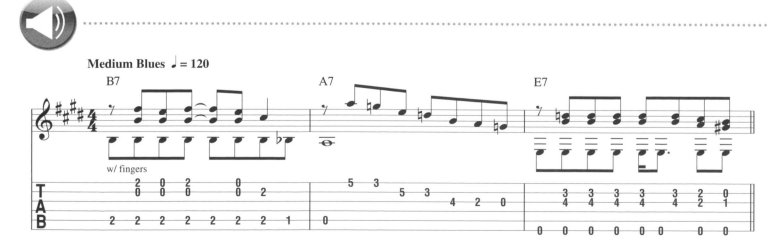

# GATEMOUTH BROWN

**Clarence "Gatemouth" Brown** (1924–2005) is one of the most important pioneers of electric Texas blues guitar and one of the first to play loud and distorted in front of a big band. His classic Peacock label recordings (1949–61) are required listening and include the seminal "Okie Dokie Stomp," "Dirty Work at the Crossroads," and "Just Before Dawn," featuring his amazing bluesy fiddle. Never wanting to be pigeonholed as a bluesman, Brown would try his hand at country music in the seventies, and his later albums would include jazz standards and older pop tunes, as well as blues. Even into his seventies, his live shows were awesome, as he could still play swing tunes at a blistering tempo that had his younger sidemen sweating to keep up.

## The Sound

In 1947, Brown played a new Gibson L-5 through a Bogan hi-fi amp with two 15" speakers, and in the fifties he switched to an early Fender Telecaster. In 1966, he began using his iconic Gibson non-reverse Firebird V with two stock mini-humbuckers, and his sound got noticeably cleaner compared to his Peacock records. In later years, he played through a 35-watt KJL amp with 10" and 12" Celestion speakers.

**Guitar:** 1966 Firebird V, **early-fifties Fender Telecaster**

**Amp:** 35-watt KJL with Celestion speakers

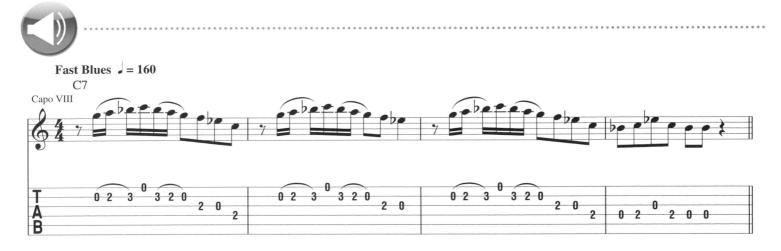

19

# JIMMY BRYANT

© R.A. Andreas / Cache Agency

**John Ivy "Jimmy" Bryant** (1925–1980) was arguably the best of the super-hot country pickers who emerged in the fifties. He acquired his flatpicking chops by being forced (by his father) to practice the fiddle. While convalescing in Washington, D.C. from injuries sustained during WWII, he met jazz guitarist Tony Mottola, who encouraged him to play guitar. By 1950, he was into country music in Southern California when Leo Fender brought him Telecaster #1 to endorse. Their relationship would last for years, only interrupted around 1953 when Fender named his new three-pickup guitar "the Stratocaster" instead of the "Jimmy Bryant Special." However, Bryant would go on to have a long, productive career backing country and western stars and recording spectacular, jaw-dropping instrumentals with his partner, steel guitarist Speedy West.

## The Sound

Bryant picked fast with a clear, bright sound colored by a hint of harmonic distortion that allowed for the clean articulation of his numerous notes. Besides Telecasters, he played the unusual 1953 Stratosphere Twin 6/12 solidbody electric through a late-forties Fender Pro amp.

**Guitar:** Fender Telecaster
**Amp:** Late-forties Fender Pro

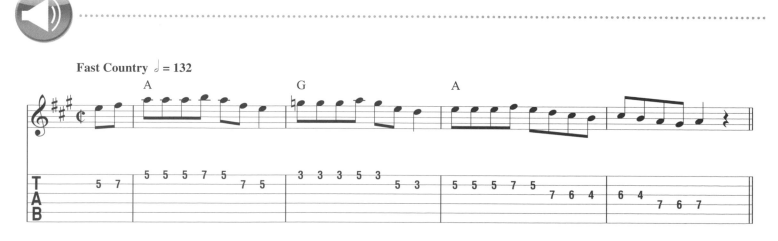

# ROY BUCHANAN

Once called "the world's greatest unknown guitar player," **Leroy "Roy" Buchanan** (1939–1988) could plumb his deepest feelings through the strings of his Telecaster while performing feats of magic with his fingers. He went on the road with Dale Hawkins from 1956–58 before settling in the Washington, D.C. area in 1960, and by the late sixties, he had become an underground guitar hero. When a documentary about him was produced in 1971, a record contract with Polydor Records resulted in the sensational *Second Album* (1972). From 1975–87, he languished at Atlantic Records before making excellent "comeback" albums for Alligator Records (and developing a cocaine habit). In 1988, after being arrested for public intoxication, he was found hanging in his jail cell—dead of an apparent suicide.

## The Sound

A naturally-overdriven tube amp tone with edge and sustain characterized the Buchanan sound throughout his career. Though he once dallied with a late-fifties Les Paul Special and newer Fender Telecasters near the end of his life, he will forever be identified with his 1953 Tele, crying through a black-face, Pre-CBS Fender Vibrolux amp.

**Guitar:** 1953 Fender Telecaster ("Nancy")
**Amp:** Pre-CBS Fender Vibrolux

© Photofest

Slow Blues ♩. = 72

# KENNY BURRELL

Duke Ellington called **Kenneth Earl "Kenny" Burrell** (1931– ) his favorite guitarist. Burrell so thoroughly melded jazz and blues that he virtually created a new style of guitar in the fifties on albums such as *Blue Moods*, *Bluesin' Around*, *Midnight Blue*, and *Blues - The Common Ground*. Coming from the funky R&B and jazz scene in Detroit, he moved to New York in 1956; this move resulted in numerous sessions in a variety of styles. Recordings with Hammond B3 organ master Jimmy Smith would be especially influential. From 1969–71, he managed a NYC club named Guitar, and in 1973, he relocated to Southern California where he currently resides and teaches. In 2001, he released *Lucky So and So* where he sings as well as plays his usual supremely silky smooth jazz.

© Andrew Lepley

## The Sound

Burrell has played a number of big "jazz box" guitars, including a 1956 Gibson ES-175 with P-90 pickups, a sixties Gibson Super 400 with humbucking pickups and Florentine (sharp) cutaway, a 1953 D'Angelico New Yorker, a custom Benedetto archtop, and a Heritage Kenny Burrell Groovemaster. For amps, a tweed Fender Deluxe, sixties Fender blackface Twin Reverb, and Heritage 45-watt Kenny Burrell model tube amp with 10" or 12" Jensen have sufficed.

**Guitar:** Sixties Gibson Super 400
**Amp:** Pre-CBS Fender Twin

# JAMES BURTON

Born on the swampy Gulf Coast of Louisiana, **James Burton** (1939– ) may have invented country rock. In 1957, he played on Dale Hawkins' "Susie-Q." A trip to Hollywood with Bob Luman resulted in Ricky Nelson snaring them for back-up on his parents' hit TV show, "The Adventures of Ozzie & Harriet," where he would turn on aspiring pickers from 1958–64. He also lent his unique, squawky "chicken pickin'" to the Bakersfield Sound in the late sixties and backed Elvis from 1969 until the King's death in 1977. Burton has only released two solo albums to date: *Corn Pickin' and Slick Slidin'* (1969) and *The Guitar Sounds of James Burton* (1971). In 2001, he was inducted into the Rock and Roll Hall of Fame.

## The Sound

Similar to Roy Buchanan, Burton honed his bright, signature, "squawking" sound with natural tube amp harmonic distortion on a 1953 Fender Telecaster through a variety of Fender amps: Deluxe, Twin, and Vibrosonic with a 15" JBL speaker. In 1969, however, Fender issued a paisley-finished Tele in his honor and he has sported it ever since. With Elvis, he played an AIMS amp that was built by former Fender employees in the seventies.

> **Guitar:** 1969 paisley Fender Telecaster
> **Amp:** Fender black-face Twin Reverb

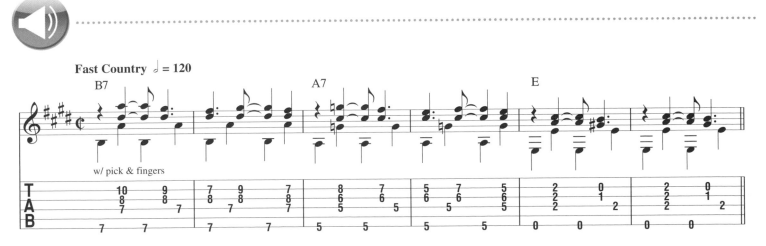

# LARRY CARLTON

© Craig Lovell / Eagle Visions Photography / Alamy

**Larry Eugene Carlton** (1948– ) was a hot session man in Los Angeles in the seventies and eighties, appearing on as many as 500 record dates a year with his melodic and bluesy style. He played with the jazz fusion group the Crusaders from 1971–76 while making countless other studio dates. Following his stunning playing on Steely Dan's *The Royal Scam*, he released his first, self-titled solo album in 1978. He won a Grammy in 1981 for the theme song of "Hill Street Blues" while releasing Grammy-nominated solo albums throughout the decade. In 1988, he was the victim of gun violence at his studio near Burbank, but heroically recovered and picked up his career in the nineties, recording solo albums and contributing to choice session work.

## The Sound

Carlton and his liquid, legato, volume-pedal sound was so identified with the Gibson ES-335 that he was literally called "Mr. 335." A 1968 sunburst model that he bought new in 1969 was used with a tweed Fender Deluxe amp on *The Royal Scam*. He has since added Seymour Duncan '57 Classic pickups to the guitar. Gibson has released a signature 335 based on his '68 axe. He also plays a Valley Arts 00-Acoustic.

**Guitar:** 1968 Gibson ES-335

**Amp:** Tweed Fender Deluxe

**Effects:** Sho-Bud volume pedal, Dunlop Cry Baby wah pedal, Roland SDE-3000, and TC Electronic M2000 with chorus and delay

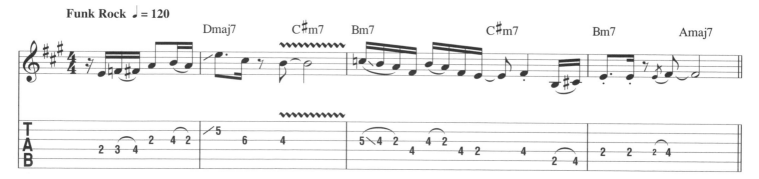

# CHARLIE CHRISTIAN

It would be impossible to overestimate the vast influence of Oklahoma jazzman **Charles Henry "Charlie" Christian** (1916–1942). He began experimenting with the electric guitar in 1937, studying with Eddie Durham and becoming the first jazz cat to successfully exploit its potential. In 1939, John Hammond, Sr. arranged an audition with Benny Goodman who was impressed with his improvisation on "Rose Room." For the next two years, he was a featured soloist in the Goodman band, making guitar history on his showcases "Flying Home" and "Solo Flight." Before he died of tuberculosis at age 25, he helped pioneer bebop by jamming at Minton's Playhouse in Harlem with Thelonious Monk and Dizzy Gillespie, among others. In 1990, he was posthumously inducted into the Rock and Roll Hall of Fame.

## The Sound

Post-war jazz guitarists would often have the "Charlie Christian pickup" from the ES-150 installed on their guitars decades after his death, and indeed, even John Lennon had one put on his late-fifties Les Paul Jr. Christian mated his ES-150 with the Gibson 15-watt EH-150 amp and 12" speaker that had previously been available for lap steel guitars, which produced a honking, distorted sound. He also played the fancier Gibson ES-250.

**Guitar:** Mid-thirties Gibson ES-150, **1939 Gibson ES-250**

**Amp:** Gibson EH-150

© Lebrecht Music and Arts Photo Library / Alamy

# ERIC CLAPTON

If Nashville's Chet Atkins was "Mr. Guitar," then London's **Eric Patrick Clapton** (1945– ) should be "Mr. Blues Rock Guitar." Big Bill Broonzy, Chuck Berry, and Bo Diddley were his inspirations in 1958, and then he discovered the great post-war electric blues guitarists. He was a member of the Yardbirds in 1963 but left in 1965 for John Mayall's Bluesbreakers. While in this new group, "Clapton is God" graffiti began to surface on the streets of London. One year later, in 1966, Clapton split to form Cream. In 1970, he recorded his first solo album and then convened Derek & the Dominoes for *Layla... and Other Assorted Love Songs*. His ongoing, spectacular career was acknowledged by the Rock and Roll Hall of Fame, as he is the only triple inductee (the Yardbirds, Cream, and as a solo artist in 1992, 1993, and 2000, respectively).

## The Sound

Clapton is a trendsetter. In the Bluesbreakers, he played a 1960 Gibson Les Paul Standard through a Marshall combo amp, followed by a 1964 Gibson SG and a 1962 ES-335 in Cream and Blind Faith, respectively. A 1956 Strat starred with Derek & the Dominoes while "Blackie," a "Frankenstein" Strat, ruled the solo years. In 1987, Fender introduced an Eric Clapton Signature Strat, their first ever. Clapton favors Marshall, Fender, Music Man, and Soldano amps.

© Marty Temme

**Guitar:** 1960 Gibson Les Paul Standard, 1956 Fender Stratocaster ("Brownie"), **"Frankenstein" Fender Stratocaster ("Blackie")**

**Amp:** Marshall JTM 45, Fender Dual Showman

**Effects:** Vox Cry Baby wah pedal, Leslie, Dallas Arbiter Fuzz Face, Dallas Rangefinder Treble Booster

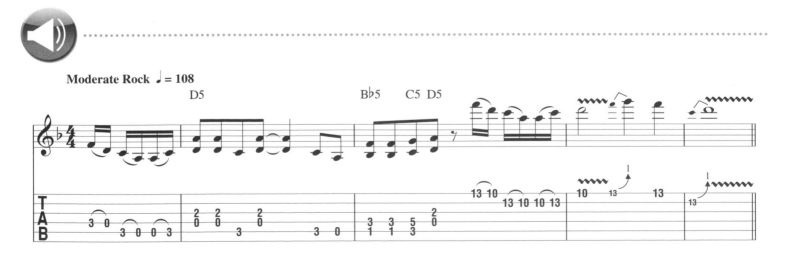

# KURT COBAIN

**Kurt Cobain** (1967–1994) had a difficult childhood in a broken home in Washington state. He bought his first guitar at 14, initially influenced by the Beatles, the Monkees and then KISS, Black Sabbath, and the Sex Pistols. After dropping out of high school, he formed Nirvana in 1986 with bassist Krist Novaselic and various drummers; the band released *Bleach* in 1989. Adding permanent drummer Dave Grohl to the lineup, Nirvana broke out with the #1 album *Nevermind* in 1991, containing hit singles "Smells Like Teen Spirit" (#6), "Come as You Are" (#3), and "Lithium" (#64), bringing melodic alternative music into the mainstream. After *Incesticide* (1992) and *In Utero* (1993), Cobain was found dead from a gunshot wound on April 8, 1994.

## The Sound

Emblematic of the Seattle grunge sound, the left-handed Cobain reveled in the rawest of overdriven tones. He brutalized Fender Mustangs and Jaguars fitted with humbuckers, followed by Strats and Teles that were often Japanese- or Mexican-made copies. Rackmount amplification and Fender, Vox, and Peavey combo amps were part of a large selection of gear. Along with pervasive amp distortion, Cobain was fond of effects, including chorus and distortion stomp boxes.

© Marty Temme

**Guitar:** 1969 "Lake Placid Blue" Fender Mustang, sunburst 1965 Fender Jaguar, 1991 Fender Stratocaster with bridge humbucker, **custom "Sonic Blue" Mustang**, 1992 custom Danny Ferrington Mustang, Harmony 12-string (with only five nylon strings)

**Amp:** Mesa Boogie Studio preamp with Crown power amp and Marshall 4x12 cabinets, Mesa Boogie Studio .22, Fender Bassman, Vox AC30

**Effects:** Boss DS-1 distortion; Electro-Harmonix Big Muff, Small Clone chorus, and Polychorus; Tech 21 Sans Amp Classic; ProCo Rat

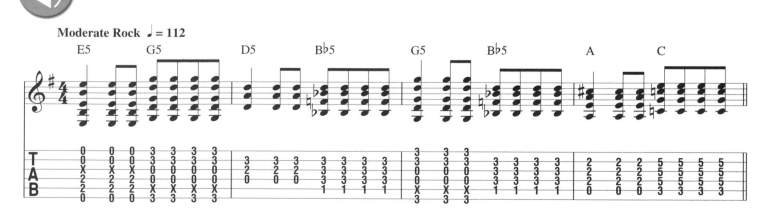

# RY COODER

© Warner Bros Records / Reprise / Photofest

**Ryland Peter Cooder** (1947– ) is the Renaissance man of folk music. The Los Angelino has played virtually all forms of American roots music, as well as reggae, Tex-Mex, classic Indian, and Cuban music. At 16, he was in a blues band with Jackie DeShannon and later formed Rising Sons with Taj Mahal. He became a session guitarist specializing in slide, appearing on the Rolling Stones' *Let It Bleed* (1969). In the seventies, he released *Paradise and Lunch* (1974), *Chicken Skin Music* (1976), and *Bop Till You Drop* (1979)—the latter being the first digital major-label release. In the eighties, he began playing on movie soundtracks, and in the 2000s he released his first solo albums since 1987 with *Chavez Ravine* (2005), *My Name is Buddy* (2007), and *I, Flathead* (2008).

## The Sound

Cooder has played a sometimes wacky assortment of stringed instruments and is revered for his tone. His axes include a 1967 Strat modified with a Bigsby tremolo bar and replacement pickups, a CBS Strat for slide with an Oahu horse shoe pickup, and a thirties Gibson Roy Smeck model. A fifties Gibson GA-40, fifties Flot-A-Tone, Magnatone Custom 280 High Fidelity head, and a Standel 25L 15 Vintage Plus drive his sound.

> **Guitar:** 1967 Fender Stratocaster
>
> **Amp:** Fifties Gibson GA-40
>
> **Effects:** Dan Armstrong Orange Squeezer

# STEVE CROPPER

**Stephen Lee "The Colonel" Cropper** (1941– ) is one of the most influential rhythm guitarists. He began playing guitar in Memphis at 14, influenced by Chet Atkins, Tal Farlow, Chuck Berry, and Lowman Pauling of the 5 Royales. In 1961, his high school band, the Mar-Keys, recorded the #3 instrumental single "Last Night" for the new Stax label, and he became their engineer and A&R man. With Booker T & the MGs, he had a #3 instrumental hit with "Green Onions" (1962) and began backing Otis Redding, Wilson Pickett, Eddie Floyd, Sam & Dave, and Albert King. Ironically, his highest visibility was with the comedic Blues Brothers. Booker T & the MGs were inducted into the Rock and Roll Hall of Fame in 1992.

## The Sound

One of the world's great Tele players with a distinct "spanky" tone, Cropper made his bones with a 1959 Esquire that he sanded down, painted purple, and played through a late-fifties tweed Fender Harvard amp. Around 1962, he bought a new, white Telecaster that he would often hook up to a pre-CBS Fender Super Reverb. In 1998, Peavey introduced a Cropper Classic Signature Tele-style guitar.

© Stax Record Co. / Photofest

**Guitar:** 1962 Fender Telecaster

**Amp:** Mid-fifties Fender Harvard

Moderate Funk ♩ = 112

# DICK DALE

While he did not invent surf music, **Richard Anthony Monsour** (1937– ) contributed more than anyone else. Born to Lebanese/Polish parents in Boston, he would incorporate Middle Eastern melodies in his instrumental classics such as "Misirlou" (1962). After his family moved to Southern California in 1954, he developed an interest in surfing and wanted to capture the sound in his music, which resulted in the outboard reverb tank and the powerful Showman amp created in conjunction with Leo Fender. The British Invasion would derail his career until his 1986 duet with Stevie Ray Vaughan on "Pipeline" from the soundtrack of *Back to the Beach*, though his biggest break was having "Misirlou" featured on the soundtrack of *Pulp Fiction* in 1994. In 2001, *Spacial Disorientation* was released.

## The Sound

Dale plays exceptionally loud and clean. In 1955, Leo Fender gave him a right-handed Strat that he turned upside down and played backwards. Together, they developed the Showman and Dual Showman amps with heavy duty JBL D130F (the "D" stood for Dale; the "F" stood for Fender) speakers that would stand up to his pounding bass string attack. In 1994, Fender introduced the Dick Dale Signature Strat that is not an exact copy.

© Marty Temme

**Guitar:** 1955 Fender Stratocaster, **Pre-CBS Fender chartreuse sparkle Stratocaster**

**Amp:** Early-sixties Fender Dual Showman

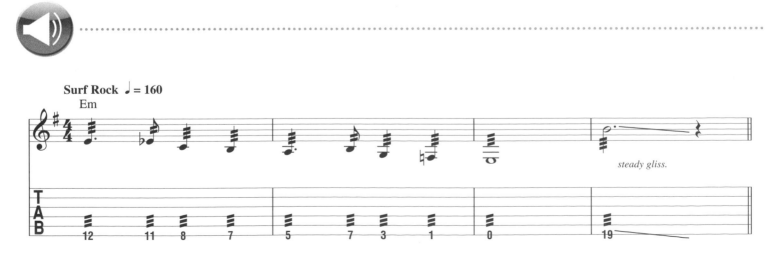

# DIMEBAG DARRELL

© Marty Temme

**Guitar: Dean ML model** and Dime O'Flame

**Amp:** Randall RG 100ES

**Effects:** MXR 6-band graphic equalizer and 126 Flanger/Doubler, Zack Wylde Overdrive, Boss CE-1 Chorus, Electro-Harmonix Electric Mistress, EBow, Dunlop 535Q Cry Baby from Hell (co-designed by Darrell), Dunlop Octave Fuzz and Wah

**Darrell Lance Abbott** (1966–2004) abandoned his Texas roots when he discovered KISS and started playing at age 12. In 1981, as "Diamond Darrell," he formed the glam metal band Pantera with his brother, drummer Vinnie Paul, and released *Metal Magic* (1983), *Projects in the Jungle* (1984), *I Am the Night* (1985), and *Power Metal* (1988). A change of direction to groove metal with *Cowboys from Hell* (1990), *Vulgar Display of Power* (1992), and *Far Beyond Driven* (1994) propelled them to the upper reaches of metal stardom. However, following *The Great Southern Trendkill* (1996), *Official Live: 100 Proof* (1997), and *Reinventing the Steel* (2000), Darrell and Vinnie formed Damageplan and released *New Found Power* (2004). Incredibly and tragically, Darrell was shot dead while performing on stage in Columbus, Ohio by a delusional Pantera fan.

## The Sound

From 1980–94 Darrell played the Dean ML model with Bill Lawrence L500XL pickups until Dean went out of business. He played a number of Washburn signature guitars including the 333 Dimebag Darrell, Culprit Dimebag, and Stealth Dimebag, and then followed Dean back into business in late 2004; this later collaboration resulted in the Dime O'Flame. He employed a variety of solid state Randall amps over the years, followed by Krank Revolution tube heads and cabinets.

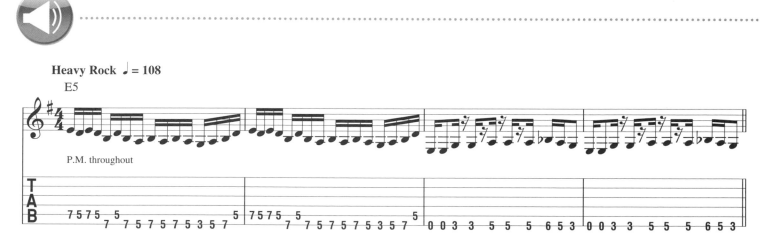

Heavy Rock ♩ = 108

E5

P.M. throughout

# BO DIDDLEY

© Marty Temme

Mississippian **Ellas Bates** (1928–2008) (later Ellas McDaniel and then Bo Diddley), is lauded for inventing the "Bo Diddley beat." With roots in Africa, it would be adapted by many others. By the early fifties, he had a group in Chicago with guitarist Jody Williams, harmonist Billy Boy Arnold, and significantly, maracas player Jerome Green. A contract with Chess Records produced the landmark "Bo Diddley" b/w "I'm a Man" in 1955, followed by "You Don't Love Me," "Diddley Daddy," "Pretty Thing," "Diddy Wah Diddy," "Who Do You Love," and others. He influenced the British Invasion in the sixties as his own creativity and commercial success waned. In 1989, he appeared with baseball star Bo Jackson in a popular TV commercial built around the phrase "Bo knows."

## The Sound

Diddley, a creative and inveterate tinkerer, built his own rhomboidal-shaped guitar in 1945 when he was 17. In the early sixties, he used a 1955–60 tweed Fender Bassman and then a pre-CBS Fender Dual Showman connected to his famous Gretsch square-body guitar called the "Big B," originally built in 1958. The Cadillac fin models followed a few years later. His classic tracks often have raw tube distortion combined with tremolo.

**Guitar:** 1958 Gretsch G6138, **1992 Kinman "The Mean Machine"**

**Amp:** Tweed Fender Bassman

**Effects:** DeArmond model 60 Tremolo Control

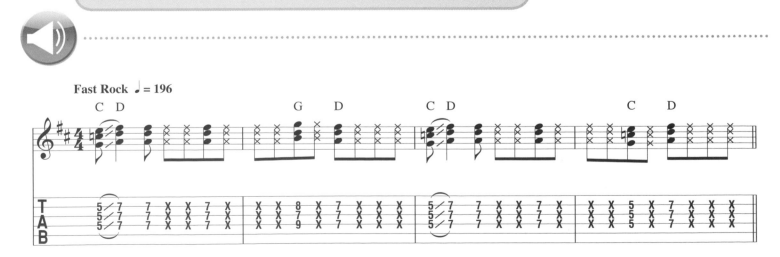

# AL DI MEOLA

Once considered the world's fastest guitarist, **Al Laurence Di Meola** (1954– ) evolved beyond blazing fusion chops. Originally from New Jersey, Di Meola briefly attended the Berklee School of Music before joining Return to Forever at age 19 in 1974. Shortly thereafter, *Where Have I Known You Before* (1974) and *No Mystery* (1975) won Grammy Awards. After *Romantic Warrior* (1976) hit the Top 40, Di Meola began a solo career with *Land of the Midnight Sun* (1976), *Elegant Gypsy, Casino* (1977), and *Splendido Hotel* (1979), and he regularly won guitar magazine reader polls. With his acoustic ensemble, World Sinfonia, he turned to acoustic Latin and world music in 1990. *Diabolic Inventions and Seductions for Solo Guitar, Vol. 1: Music of Astor Piazolla* (2007) explores the nuevo tango style of the Argentinean composer.

## The Sound

Di Meola initially slung a 1959 burst refinished in black (!) with DiMarzio Super Distortion humbuckers as his iconic axe with Return to Forever and in his early solo career. Gibson has released a Signature Al Di Meola Les Paul and an L-5. Marshall stacks gave him plenty of wattage with Return to Forever, but over the years he has downsized to combos such as the 50-watt Mesa Boogie Stiletto Ace.

© C. Taylor Crothers

**Guitar:** 1959 Gibson Les Paul
**Amp:** Marshall 100-watt stack

# CORNELL DUPREE

One of the greatest Texas guitarists, **Cornell Luther Dupree** (1942–2011) built upon the blues to become the premier R&B guitarist of his generation. In 1961, tenor saxman King Curtis heard him and advised, "Keep on practicing, and one of these days I will send for you." The call came a year later, and Dupree was auditioned over the phone by playing the saxophonist's hit, "Soul Twist." His signature playing on Brook Benton's hit version of "Rainy Night in Georgia" (1969) made his tasty fills a valuable commodity. Dupree recorded his solo debut, *Teasin'*, in 1973 and formed the instrumental juggernaut, Stuff, in 1975 and played with them through to 1979. He also was a member of a revamped version as the Gadd Gang from 1985–86. In the nineties, Dupree released a series of solo albums.

## The Sound

Dupree tried a late-fifties Gibson Les Paul Jr., early seventies Guild Starfire, and a Standel. He switched to a CBS Fender Telecaster around 1970, and the bright, clean sparkle became his sound through CBS Fender Twin Reverb amps. He later played a Yamaha Tele-style Dupree SJ-800 with a Yamaha humbucker in the neck position and a single-coil pickup in the bridge. Before passing away in 2011, he favored a Fender "red knob" Twin Reverb amp.

© Andrew Lepley

> **Guitar:** Fender CBS Telecaster,
> **Yamaha Pacifica Dupree SJ-800**
>
> **Amp:** Fender Twin Reverb

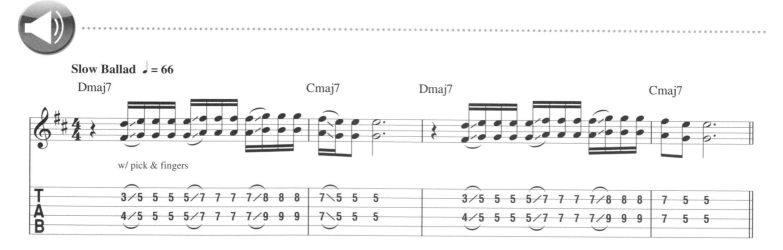

# DUANE EDDY

**Duane Eddy** (1938– ) had to play "down" for the instrumentals that made him famous. He moved from New York state to Arizona in 1951, and met local DJ and producer Lee Hazlewood, who had him play simple, twangy riffs on the bottom strings with deep echo. He entered the Top 40 fifteen times through to 1963, starting with "Moovin' 'n' Groovin'" and highlighted by the #6 hit "Rebel Rouser" (both in 1958). In 1986 he re-recorded "Peter Gunn" with the Art of Noise and received a Grammy for Best Rock Instrumental. In 1987, Eddy played on Paul McCartney's "Rockestra Theme" in addition to having a raft of rock stars guesting on his self-titled comeback album. He was inducted into the Rock and Roll Hall of Fame in 1994.

## The Sound

Eddy was the first rock guitarist to have a signature guitar when Guild introduced the DE-400 and DE-500 models in 1962. Prior to that, he had been mainly associated with a 1957 Gretsch 6120 model that was issued in 1997 as the 6120-DE Signature Model, and in 2004, Gibson produced a Duane Eddy Signature guitar. He played a Magnatone amp, reportedly modified to 100 watts, on most of his classic recordings.

© William "Popsie" Randolph

**Guitar:** 1957 Gretsch 6120, Guild Duane Eddy DE-400 and DE-500 Signature models

**Amp:** Magnatone 280

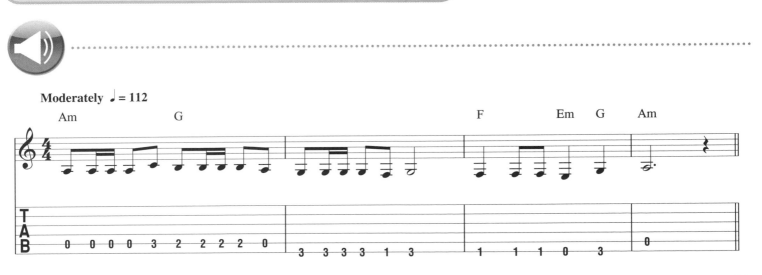

Moderately ♩ = 112

# THE EDGE

© David Atlas / Retna Ltd. USA

English guitarist **David Howell "The Edge" Evans** (1961– ) is the instrumental driving force behind the Irish rock band U2. He built his own guitar and began playing in high school, joining the band as it formed in 1976 as the Feedback after responding to an ad on the school bulletin board. *Boy* debuted in 1980, and in 1987, *The Joshua Tree,* their first #1 record in the U.S., made them superstars. Through a constant evolution of their music from politics to dance rock and back to straight rock with *How to Dismantle an Atomic Bomb* (2004) that won eight Grammys, U2 remains enormously popular down to the current day. U2 was inducted into the Rock and Roll Hall of Fame in 2005.

## The Sound

The Edge was given his nickname because his mind is so sharp, according to Bono, and the same could be said for his sound. Highly processed, yet defined, with bright highs and rich lows, it plays dynamically against the basic backbeat of the U2 rhythm section. To achieve his sound, he employs extensive pedals and rackmount effects. The Edge owns a huge collection of guitars and over 30 Vox AC30 amps.

**Guitar:** 1976 Gibson Explorer

**Amp:** 1964 Vox AC30 Top Boost

**Effects:** Lovetone Doppleganger, Electro-Harmonix POG, Ibanez TS-9 Tube Screamer, Death by Audio Supersonic Fuzz Gun, Skrydstrup Bufferooster, Rocktron DVC Volume Controller, Electrix Filter Factory

Moderate Rock ♩ = 100

*w/ delay

*Set to 450 ms w/ one repeat

36

# TOMMY EMMANUEL

As Australia's answer to Chet Atkins, **William Thomas "Tommy" Emmanuel** (1955– ) is a devastating fingerstyle virtuoso. He was taught to play by his mother from the age of four. Emmanuel heard "Mr. Guitar" at age seven and wrote him a letter, beginning a longstanding friendship. Emmanuel was playing professionally by nine when his father took the whole family on the road to perform. In the seventies and eighties, Emmanuel played in a number of bands before going solo with *Up from Down Under* (1988), and in 1997, he recorded *The Day Finger Pickers Took Over the World* with Atkins—the last album by the Nashville master. In 2000, he and his brother, Phil, played the closing ceremonies of the Sydney Olympics to an estimated 2.85 billion viewers.

## The Sound

Emmanuel plays with his bare fingers, a flatpick and fingers, or a thumbpick and fingers in a style that is eclectic, but based on Travis picking as learned through Chet Atkins. His Australian-made Maton guitars, including his Signature TE 1, have pickups and condenser microphones for a full, natural, acoustic sound. He requires promoters to provide a quality, high-powered PA system with active DI boxes to amplify his guitars.

**Guitar:** Maton EBG808
**Effects:** Alesis Miniverb 4

© Daniel Coston / Retna Ltd.

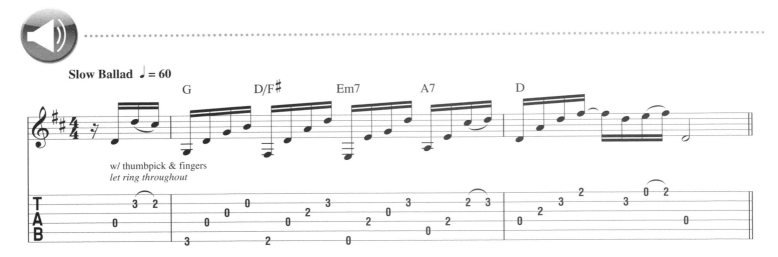

# JOHN FOGERTY

He was from Northern California and had never been near the bayou when he started mythologizing it. However, songwriter/singer/guitarist **John Cameron Fogerty** (1945– ) was able to tap into the American psyche with deep roots in southern blues, country, and folk music. He and his brother, Tom, formed the Golliwogs in the late fifties before changing their name to Creedence Clearwater Revival (CCR) in 1967. From 1968–72, they had nine Top 10 singles including "Proud Mary" and "Bad Moon Rising," and eight gold albums. The band split acrimoniously in 1971, and Fogerty went on to have a productive, if less spectacular and consistent, solo career with albums like the #1 *Centerfield* (1984). Creedence was inducted into the Rock and Roll Hall of Fame in 1993.

## The Sound

An accomplished electric and acoustic guitarist, Fogerty has played a variety of gear. In CCR, he used a Gibson J-200, Rickenbacker 325 modified with a Gibson PAF and a Bigsby whammy bar, a Gibson ES-175, and a number of Les Paul Customs that would become his primary axes. Besides his famous "rolled and pleated" Kustom amps, he also recorded with a black-face Fender Concert and a silver-face Fender Vibrolux amp.

© Robb D. Cohen / Retna Ltd.

**Guitar:** Modified 1967 Rickenbacker 325, **Gibson Les Paul Custom**
**Amp:** 1967 K-200A-4 Kustom with two 15" JBL D130 speakers

# ROBBEN FORD

California-born **Robben Lee Ford** (1951– ) is a fluid and versatile guitarist whose early training on the alto sax influenced his blues and jazz style. At 18, he formed the Charles Ford Band (named for his father) with his brother Mark and then moved on to backing Charlie Musselwhite. From 1972–77 he played with Jimmy Witherspoon, the L.A. Express, George Harrison, and Joni Mitchell. From 1977–83, he led the fusion band, the Yellowjackets, while doing sessions and solo work, including the soulful blues album *Talk to Your Daughter* (1988). In 1986, he toured with Miles Davis, but a turnaround back to the blues in 1992 resulted in his most aesthetically-satisfying period with *Blue Moon* (2002) and the live *Soul on Ten* (2009).

## The Sound

Ford's sound combines the smooth harmonies of jazz with the bite and sustain of the blues. His axes have included a Gibson Super 400, 1957 Gibson Les Paul Goldtop, 1960 Fender Telecaster, a Taku Sakashta custom, and a 1968 Gibson ES-335. He uses a Dumble Overdrive Special and 1963 and 1966 Fender Super Reverbs. He tends to use effects sparingly, except for distortion and delay.

**Guitar:** Taku Sakashta custom

**Amp:** Dumble Overdrive Special

**Effects:** Hermida Audio Zendrive, TC Electronic 2290 delay, Vox wah pedal, Ernie Ball volume pedal

© Anthony Pidgeon / Retna Ltd.

# PETER FRAMPTON

© Marty Temme

English guitarist **Peter Kenneth Frampton** (1950– ) sublimated his advanced techniques learned while studying classical music and listening to jazz as a child to become a huge rock star in 1976 with his blockbuster album, *Frampton Comes Alive!* Previously, he was in several other bands, including Humble Pie from 1969–71. Unfortunately, he was never able to achieve such a level of commercial success again and endured a series of personal setbacks as well, leaving music for a few years in the mid eighties. In the nineties, he picked up his career, and following *Now* (2004), his first studio record in nine years, he released the instrumental, Grammy-winning *Fingerprints* (2006). *Thank You, Mr. Churchill* (2010), an ambitious concept album tracing his history from WWII on, has also been well-received.

## The Sound

Frampton has been closely identified with a 1960 Les Paul Custom with three pickups that Gibson recreated and released in 2007 as a signature model. He also counts a 1958 Les Paul, Jr. and a G&L ASAT in his arsenal. Besides 100- and 50-watt Marshalls, he also uses a Mesa Boogie Mark IV and an Ampeg ET-1 Echo Twin with a "Framptone" amp switcher that allows access to four different setups.

> **Guitar:** 1960 Gibson Les Paul Custom, Tacoma Jumbo JK50
>
> **Amp:** Marshall 100-watt stack, Hammond/Suzuki Leslie
>
> **Effects:** Frampton Talk Box, Ibanez TS-9 Tube Screamer, Mu-tron Octave Divider, MXR Phase 90

# ROBERT FRIPP

The most progressive of all British rock guitarists, **Robert Fripp** (1946– ) pushes the envelope of avant-garde pop music, irrespective of trends. In England in the sixties, he played in the League of Gentlemen and Giles and Fripp, the latter of which evolved into King Crimson and produced their debut album, *In the Court of the Crimson King* (1969). After the band's breakup in 1974, Fripp retired for three years. He returned as a sideman, initiated a solo career, and reformed a new King Crimson 1981–84. His teaching of "Guitar Craft" and the release of *The League of Crafty Guitarists* (1986) with his students followed, along with solo albums. In 1994, he again reformed King Crimson. He returned to playing solo and with others in 1997 and also released an instrumental album, *Soundscapes*.

## The Sound

Fripp began conventionally enough, but eventually, he developed a system of looped tape and effects in 1977 that he dubbed "Frippertronics" (introduced to him by Brian Eno in 1972). He also developed a "new standard tuning" (see musical figure below). Fripp has employed a vast array of effects for a highly-processed sound through Marshall, Hiwatt, and Fender amps. Crimson Guitars has released a Robert Fripp Fernandez Les Paul-type signature model.

© Ebet Roberts / Redferns / Getty Images

**Guitar:** 1957 Gibson Les Paul Standard, Roland GR-300, Gibson ES-355 Stereo, **RF Les Paul-type**

**Amp:** Roland JC-120

**Effects:** Roland VG-8 synthesizer, TC Electronic TC 2290 Dynamic Digital Delay, DigiTech WH-1 Whammy pedal

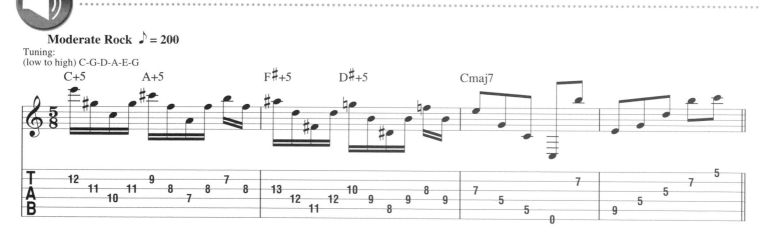

# JOHN FRUSCIANTE

**John Frusciante** (1970– ) was born in NYC and raised in California. He dropped out of high school after being inspired by the playing of Frank Zappa, King Crimson, the Germs, and Black Flag. He realized a dream when he joined the Red Hot Chili Peppers in 1988, replacing Hillel Slovak, who had recently died of a drug overdose. His funky virtuosity would contribute to the breakthrough success of *Mother's Milk* (1989) and *Blood, Sugar, Sex, Magik* (1991). However, due to a growing heroin habit, Frusciante left the Peppers in 1992. Following two solo albums, he entered rehab and rejoined the band in 1998 after the departure of Dave Navarro. The reunion produced the epic *Californication* (1999) after which he released a number of solo albums. Frusciante continued to perform with the Peppers until officially announcing his departure in 2009.

## The Sound

Frusciante plays from clean to dirty with substantial signal processing. His Strats include 1955, 1961, and 1962 models, as well as Telecasters, a Gretsch White Falcon, and a Martin D-18. Amps feature the Marshall JTM45, 200-watt Major, 100-watt Super Bass, and 2555 Silver Jubilee. Effects include a Boss CE-1 Chorus Ensemble, DS-2 Turbo Distortion, FZ-3 Fuzz, Ibanez WH10 Wah, MXR Phase 90, Electro-Harmonix Delay, Micro Synthesizer, and Big Muff Pi, among others.

© Robert Knight

**Guitar:** 1955 Fender Stratocaster

**Amp:** Marshall Silver Jubilee and Marshall Major

**Effects:** Boss CE-Chorus Ensemble and DS-Turbo Distortion, Ibanez WH10 Wah

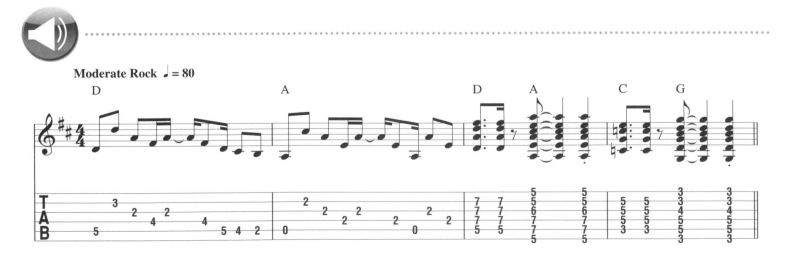

Moderate Rock ♩ = 80

# JERRY GARCIA

© Marty Temme

The father of the jam band movement, **Jerome John "Jerry" Garcia** (1942–1995) was born to a Spanish immigrant musician and an American mother in San Francisco. He began playing at 15 when he entered art school. After a dishonorable discharge from the Army in 1960, he met several of his future bandmates in Palo Alto while playing in the clubs. Forming Mother McCree's Uptown Jug Champions in 1964, they evolved from the Warlocks to the Grateful Dead by 1965 (as funded by LSD guru, Owsley Stanley). Officially beginning in the "Summer of Love" of 1967, his "long, strange trip" would last until his drug-related death in 1995, leaving some 22 albums, not including his side projects in the Jerry Garcia Band, New Riders of the Purple Sage, and solo albums.

## The Sound

Garcia produced a smooth, bright tone on a Guild Starfire III, 1957 Les Paul Custom, late-sixties Gibson SG, 1963 Strat, 1956–57 Strat ("Alligator"), 1972 Doug Irwin custom, 1973 Irwin custom ("Wolf") with GK-7 synthesizer interface, 1975 Travis Bean TB1000A, 1976 Travis Bean TB500, 1979 Irwin ("Tiger"), and 1990 Irwin ("Rosebud"). Garcia liked post-CBS twins mated with a Vox wah pedal, Mu-tron III Envelope Filter, Boss OC-2 Octave Divider, and OD-1 Turbo Overdrive.

**Guitar:** Doug Irwin "Wolf," "Tiger," and **"Rosebud"** with MIDI controls

**Amp:** Silver-face Fender Twin Reverb into McIntosh 2300 amp with three Alembic B-12 speaker cabinets

**Effects:** Vox wah, Mu-tron III Envelope Filter, MXR Distortion +

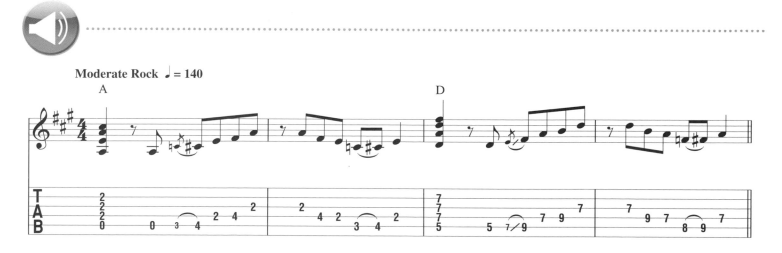

# DANNY GATTON

© Daniel Root / Retna

Like his friendly rival, Roy Buchanan, **Daniel Wood "Danny" Gatton, Jr.** (1945–1994) was known as the "world's greatest unknown guitar player." Unfortunately, it also reflected the lack of commercial success for the Washington, D.C. native. Possibly the greatest electric guitar virtuoso ever, he was feared as "The Humbler" for his ability to play effortlessly in virtually any style of popular music. But his lack of vocals confounded the record labels, and he backed Roger Miller and Robert Gordon before releasing critically-acclaimed instrumental albums including *Unfinished Business* (1978), *88 Elmira St.* (1991), *New York Stories* (1992), *Cruisin' Deuces* (1993), and *Relentless* (1994, with jazz organist Joey DeFrancesco). Following the death of his friend, Billy Windsor, and growing despondency, he committed suicide (like Buchanan) in the fall of 1994.

## The Sound

Gatton often modified his guitars. Prior to acquiring his classic 1953 Telecaster, Gatton played, among others, a 1956 Gibson ES-350T, a circa-1960 Les Paul Custom, and three Custom Shop prototype Teles before Fender introduced a signature 1953 model in 1990 and a Custom Shop double-neck Tele (six string and six-string bass) in 1994. Gatton liked vintage tweed and black-face Fender amps and used few effects beyond an Echoplex or Chandler digital echo.

**Guitar:** Modified 1953 Fender Telecaster with Joe Barden pickups

**Amp:** Circa-1956 tweed Fender Twin with EV SRO speakers

**Effects:** Homemade "Magic Dingus box" that originally controlled an Echoplex, amp reverb and vibrato, phase shifters, and a Leslie that attached to the guitar

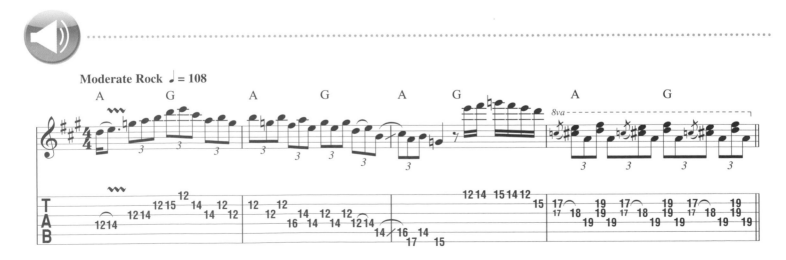

# BILLY GIBBONS

The "Reverend Willy G," born **William Frederick Gibbons** (1949– ) in Texas, is one of the blues-rock guitar greats. He began playing at 13 and gravitated from rock 'n' roll to the blues via his black housekeeper. Jimi Hendrix publicly praised him for his work in the psychedelic Moving Sidewalks, and Gibbons formed ZZ Top with Dusty Hill and Frank Beard in 1969. The longest-surviving original rock group evolved from their hard blues classics like *Tres Hombres* (1972) to their 1980s MTV days with stripped-down dance blockbusters *Eliminator* (1983) and *Afterburner* (1985)—featuring hot girls, hot rods, and long beards. They were inducted into the Rock and Roll Hall of Fame in 2004 and continue to perform while planning to record.

## The Sound

Gibbons is an addicted "gearhead" with a 1959 Les Paul, 1958 Strat (a gift from Hendrix), 1958 Les Paul (for slide), 1958 Gibson Flying V, 1951 Fender Esquire, 1959 Gretsch Jupiter Thunderbird, and custom "fuzzy" guitars played through a variety of Fender, Marshall, Vox, Crate, and Jake Stack Rio Grande amps. Selected effects include a Vox Cry Baby wah, Bionix Expandora, Jake Stack Bizarktone, Roland Chorus, Lexicon Digital Reverb, and MXR Pitch Transposer.

© Marty Temme

**Guitar:** 1959 Gibson Les Paul ("Pearly Gates"), 1958 Fender Stratocaster

**Amp:** Marshall 18-watt 2x12 combo, Super Lead Plexi 100-watt, and JCM800 100-watt

**Effects:** Bixonic Expandora distortion, Jake Stack Bizarktone, Vox Cry Baby wah

# PAUL GILBERT

**Paul Brandon Gilbert** (1966– ) was a child prodigy from Illinois who was performing professionally at 15 and featured in Guitar Player magazine as a new heavy metal star. He attended the Guitar Institute of Technology (GIT) in L.A. in 1984 and became an instructor one year later. After forming Electric Fence, which evolved into Racer X, Gilbert gained a reputation as "the fastest shredder." In 1987, after two albums, he joined Mr. Big, who had a #1 pop hit with "To Be With You" in 1992. Following the band's split in 1996, Gilbert commenced a solo career, starting with *King of Clubs* (1997), and produced at least one album almost every year through to *Fuzz Universe* (2010). In 2009, Mr. Big reunited for a tour.

## The Sound

Gilbert does not use excessive distortion or a whammy bar. He plays Ibanez guitars, including his signature PGM300 and PGM301, RG750, and a "Fireman" that he designed. After using ADA preamps and Ampeg and Marshall amps, he switched to Laney tube amps and then Marshall Vintage Modern 2266C combo amps. Gilbert uses few effects (ADA Flanger and Boss DD-3 Digital Delay), but has been known to attach guitar picks to a cordless drill!

© Marty Temme

**Guitar:** Ibanez Signature **PGM300**, RG750 ("Dino")
**Amp:** Metaltronix head, ADA preamp, Ampeg V4 head
**Effects:** ADA Flanger, Boss DD-3 Digital Delay, Dunlop Cry Baby wah

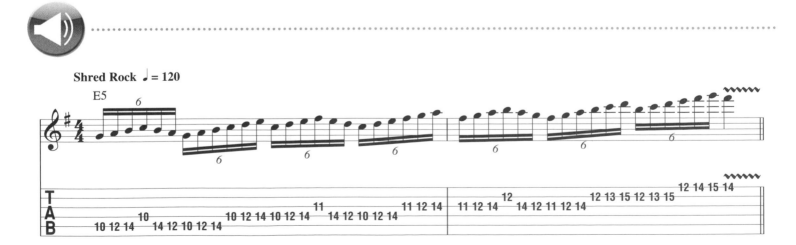

# DAVID GILMOUR

English rocker **David Jon Gilmour** (1944– ) is best known for his inventive playing with Pink Floyd during their most productive period (1968–87). Originally brought in to cover for the mentally-unbalanced Syd Barrett (1946–2006), he soon became a permanent replacement. With bassist/songwriter/vocalist Roger Waters and Gilmour leading the way, Floyd would go from psychedelic to progressive rock and achieve superstardom following *Dark Side of the Moon* (1973). In 1986, Waters sued Gilmour and drummer Nick Mason for control of the band and lost, which lead to his departure. Floyd continued through *The Division Bell* (1994) with varying degrees of success under Gilmour's leadership and reunited at Live 8 in 2005. He has released four successful solo albums from *David Gilmour* (1978) to *Live in Gdansk* (2008).

## The Sound

Gilmour is a Strat man. He owns a custom model with serial #0001 from 1954, along with 1969, 1957 reissue (1984), 1957, and 1959 models, and other guitars including a Bill Lewis Custom used for *Dark Side of the Moon* and *The Wall*. Fender issued two signature model Strats in 2008. Hiwatt, Fender, and Marshalls have been his main amps, and his many effects include Electro-Harmonix, MXR, Boss, and Pete Cornish pedals.

© Marty Temme

**Guitar:** 1969 Fender Stratocaster with 1957 reissue "C" neck, Bill Lewis 24-fret custom

**Amp:** Hiwatt DR-103 head with WEM Super Starfinder 200 with 4x12 cabinets, 1956 tweed Fender Twin, Fender Twin Reverb

**Effects:** Electro-Harmonix Big Muff and Electric Mistress Phaser, Dallas Arbiter Fuzz Face

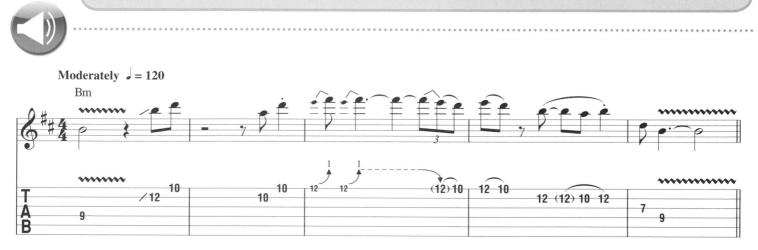

# PETER GREEN

© Pictorial Press Ltd. / Alamy

**Peter Alan Greenbaum** (1946– ) is considered by many to be the greatest British blues guitarist. He took Eric Clapton's place in John Mayall's Bluesbreakers in 1966 and formed Fleetwood Mac in 1967 with drummer Mick Fleetwood, bassist John McVie, slide guitarist Jeremy Spencer, and lead guitarist Danny Kirwan. With the singles "Albatross" and "Black Magic Woman" and the album *Then Play On* (1969), Fleetwood Mac achieved popularity in England beyond that of the Beatles and Rolling Stones. Unfortunately, in 1970, following LSD abuse, Green became mentally unstable and left the band only to record sporadically over the next decades. He and Fleetwood Mac were inducted into the Rock and Roll Hall of Fame in 1998. In the last ten years, he has shown encouraging signs of recovering his vaunted skills.

## The Sound

Honored for his pure, singing tone and sensual vibrato, Green reversed the neck pickup and wiring on his 1959 sunburst Les Paul. In the process, he created a unique, funky, out-of-phase Fender-type tone (when both pickups are accessed via the middle position of the selector switch). Green also played a 1959 Strat on occasion and used a variety of Marshall, Fender, and Orange/Matamps without effects.

**Guitar: 1959 sunburst Gibson Les Paul Standard**, 1959 Fender Stratocaster, National Style O resonator

**Amp:** Marshall JTM45, Orange/Matamp, Fender Twin Reverb, Fender Dual Showman

# BUDDY GUY

The most explosive of Chicago's West Side blues guitarists, **George "Buddy" Guy** (1936– ) has influenced everyone from Jimi Hendrix to Eric Clapton and Stevie Ray Vaughan. Born in Louisiana, he went to Chicago in 1957 where winning head-cutting contests led him to Cobra Records. Guy moved over to Chess Records in 1960 as house guitarist and as a solo recording artist, and in 1965, he partnered up with harpist Junior Wells before going it alone on Vanguard Records in the late 1960s. Despite the release and critical acclaim of 1981's *Stone Crazy* and *D.J. Play My Blues*, Guy remained unsigned until *Damn Right I've Got the Blues* (1991) garnered his first Grammy. In 2005, he was inducted into the Rock and Roll Hall of Fame.

## The Sound

Guy sports a hard, biting sound and once played a 1961 Gibson Les Paul/SG Custom and a 1979 Guild Starfire IV, but has become identified with the ubiquitous Strat. In Chicago, he bought a brand new 1957 maple neck model that he blistered through a tweed Fender Bassman amp. He currently plays his signature model through a Chicago Blues Box Buddy Guy Signature 60-watt 4x10 combo patterned after the Bassman.

> **Guitar:** Fender Buddy Guy Signature Stratocaster
>
> **Amp:** 60-watt Chicago Blues Box Buddy Guy Signature model
>
> **Effects:** Jim Dunlop Buddy Guy BG-95 wah pedal

© Marty Temme

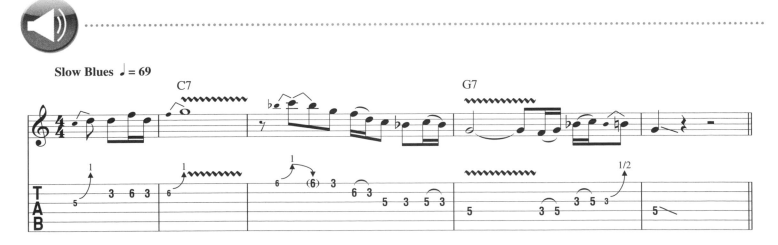

# JIM HALL

One of the great, cool, post-bop jazz guitarists, **James Stanley Hall** (1930–2013) would become a fixture on the NYC jazz scene in the early 1960s. Hall grew up in Buffalo, NY, attended the Cleveland Institute of Music, and eventually moved to Los Angeles where he studied classical guitar and played gigs with Chico Hamilton, Jimmy Giuffre, and Ella Fitzgerald. In New York, he worked with Sonny Rollins, Art Farmer, Bill Evans, Paul Desmond, and Ron Carter, among others. He was particularly adept in duo environments. In later years, he was honored as a composer, and in 1997, he was awarded the New York Critics' Circle Award for Best Jazz Composer/Arranger. He cut *Hemispheres* (2008) with his former guitar student, Bill Frisell, and recorded an album with drummer Joey Baron in 2010.

## The Sound

Hall came from the clean, low-volume, "woody" acoustic/electric jazz guitar school, but is not above using effects judiciously for orchestration. He was the opposite of a "gear head" however, though he chose his equipment with care and discrimination. Older Gibson tube amps and hollowbody archtops were his sonic tools of choice in addition to the classic Polytone jazz amp, and more recently, pedals such as distortion and chorus.

**Guitar:** Early-fifties Gibson ES-175, **D'Aquisto custom hollowbody**, D'Aquisto Avant-Garde acoustic, Sadowsky Signature model

**Amp:** Gibson GA-50, Polytone Mini-Brute

**Effects:** Boss Chorus, Alesis Microverb, Digitech EX-7 Expression Factory

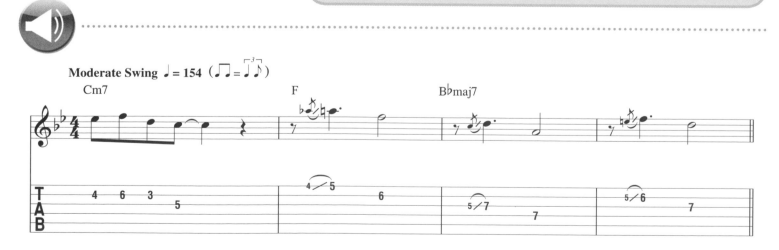

50

# GEORGE HARRISON

© Bert Kaempfert Music – K & K / Redferns / Getty Images

The "quiet Beatle," **George Harrison** (1943–2001) had a tremendous effect on would-be guitarists who tuned in to see the top British Invasion band on TV in 1964. Likewise, his extraordinarily tasteful rockabilly, psychedelic, and sitar licks and solos, plus his catalog of classic compositions like "I Want to Tell You," "While My Guitar Gently Weeps," "Here Comes the Sun," and "Something," stand up well against the Lennon/McCartney hit machine. Following the breakup of the Beatles in 1970, Harrison had a long solo career and played in the Traveling Wilburys (1988–90) with Bob Dylan, Roy Orbison, Tom Petty, and Jeff Lynne. He died of lung cancer on November 29, 2001 in Los Angeles and was posthumously inducted into the Rock and Roll Hall of Fame in 2004.

## The Sound

As the Beatles' music evolved, Harrison followed with his gear and technique. He played Gretsch guitars à la Chet Atkins and Duane Eddy, but also a 1957 Les Paul Goldtop (a gift from Eric Clapton), a 1961 Strat, and Epiphone and Rickenbacker instruments including the electric 12-string that he popularized. Harrison used few effects, including a volume pedal, fuzz tone, and Leslie through a succession of Vox and Fender amps.

**Guitar:** **1957 Gretsch Duo Jet**, 1963 Gretsch Country Gentleman, 1964 Rickenbacker 360/12, 1966 Epiphone Casino, sitar

**Amp:** Vox AC30, AC50, AC100, and Super Beatle, Fender Showman

**Effects:** Vox Tonebender, Vox Cry Baby wah, Dallas Arbiter Fuzz Face

# WARREN HAYNES

© Marty Temme

Originally drawn to soul singers, blues and rock virtuoso **Warren Haynes** (1960– ) did not start playing until hearing Cream at age 12. Working with David Allan Coe from 1980–84 provided invaluable experience and the chance to meet Dickey Betts and Gregg Allman. Both Betts and Allman called on him to play on their solo albums, and when the Allman Brothers Band reformed for their reunion tour in 1989, Haynes got tapped to join alongside Betts. Twenty-one years later, he has been a "Brother" longer than Duane. In addition, he has made a respected name for himself with his band Gov't Mule (1994–present), as a member of the Dead, and with countless other jams and gigs to which he adds his fire.

## The Sound

Haynes likes a fat Gibson sound via reissue 1959 and 1958 Les Paul Standards, a 1961 ES-335, 1964 Firebird III, 2000 reissue 1961 SG, and a 1956–57 Les Paul TV Special. Tube amps include Cesar Diaz, Soldano, Marshall, Fender, and Gibson brands. With the Dead, his effects include a Cesar Diaz Texas Tone Ranger, Centaur Distortion, Boss OC-2 Octaver, Hughes & Kettner Rotosphere, Dunlop Cry Baby wah, and Guyatone Funky Box envelope filter.

**Guitar:** 1989 reissue 1959 Gibson Les Paul Standard with Duncan Pearly Gates pickups, 1961 Gibson ES-335

**Amp:** Cesar Diaz CD-100, Soldano SLO100, reissue Marshall 100 Super Lead Plexi (100-watt)

**Effects:** Cesar Diaz Texas Tone Ranger, Centaur Distortion, Boss OC-2 Octaver

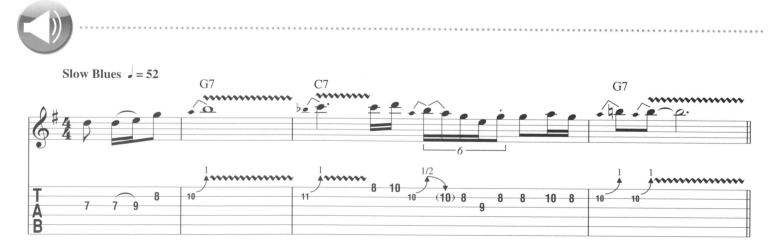

# MICHAEL HEDGES

The Windham Hill label pigeonholed him as "new age," but Oklahoma native **Michael Alden Hedges** (1953–1997) preferred "violent acoustic" to describe his virtuosic, idiosyncratic fingerstyle music. After classical training and enrollment in the electronic music program at Stanford University in 1980, Hedges was signed to Windham Hill and released *Breakfast in the Field* (1981). Critically hailed, it previewed the next evolution in acoustic fingerstyle, following Leo Kottke. *Aerial Boundaries* (1985) confirmed Hedges' status as a giant of the genre. He had dabbled with vocals, but on *The Road to Return* (1994), vocals and other instruments were prominently featured. *Oracle* (1996), his last album, was a return to acoustic, winning a Grammy for Best New Age Album. Tragically, he was killed in a car accident on December 2, 1997.

## The Sound

While mainly an acoustic player, Hedges also played electric. He often used a pick and played other instruments besides his Martin HD-28, Lowden L-250, custom Takamine, and Klein electric harp guitar. In the studio, he employed an array of electronic effects such as a TC Electronic 1140 4-band parametric equalizer and 2290 delay, Audio & Design Scamp rack, Sundholm 1/3 octave and stereo 10-band graphic equalizers, Klark Teknik DN-780 reverb, and Yamaha REV-7 and MIDI equipment.

© Andrew Lepley

**Guitar:** 1971 Martin HD-28 ("Barbara") with FRAP piezo and Sunrise magnetic pickups, Klein electric harp guitar

**Effects:** TC Electronic 1140 4-band parametric equalizer, Klark Teknik DN-780 reverb

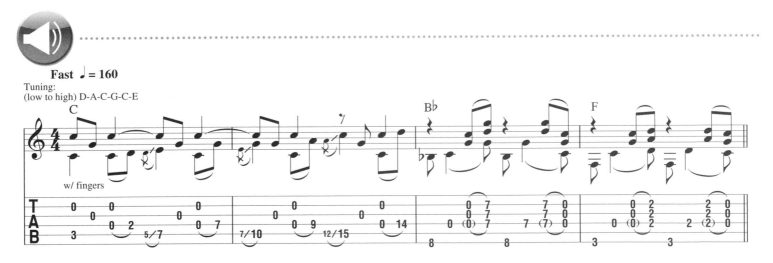

Fast ♩ = 160

Tuning:
(low to high) D-A-C-G-C-E

# JIMI HENDRIX

Seattle legend **James Marshall "Jimi" Hendrix** (1942–1970) completely revolutionized the electric guitar. Following a brief stint in the Army in 1961, he paid his dues with the Isley Brothers, Little Richard, Ike & Tina Turner, King Curtis, Curtis Knight, and John Hammond, Jr. before being introduced to Animals' bassist Chas Chandler in Greenwich Village in 1966. Chandler whisked him off to England, surrounded him with Noel Redding and Mitch Mitchell in the Experience, and the rest is history. Three landmark studio albums, *Are You Experienced?* (1967), *Axis: Bold as Love* (1967), and *Electric Ladyland* (1968) were released, followed by the unfinished *Cry of Love* (1971) before his untimely drug overdose and death on September 18, 1970. Hendrix was posthumously inducted into the Rock and Roll Hall of Fame in 1992.

## The Sound

Hendrix often played the blues, sans effects. He used right-handed CBS-era Fender Strats turned upside down and restrung them left-handed, a 1967 Gibson Flying V, custom made left-handed 1970 Flying V, 1955 Les Paul Custom, and a 1968 SG Custom; it is rumored that he used Redding's Telecaster (!) on "Purple Haze." He abused Marshall, Fender Dual Showman, and Sunn amps altered by a Dallas-Arbiter Fuzz Face, Vox Cry Baby wah, Octavia, and Univox Uni-Vibe.

> **Guitar:** Right-handed CBS-era Fender Stratocasters
>
> **Amp:** Marshall JMP Plexi 100-watt stack
>
> **Effects:** Dallas-Arbiter Fuzz Face, Vox Cry Baby wah, Octavia

© AF Archive/Alamy

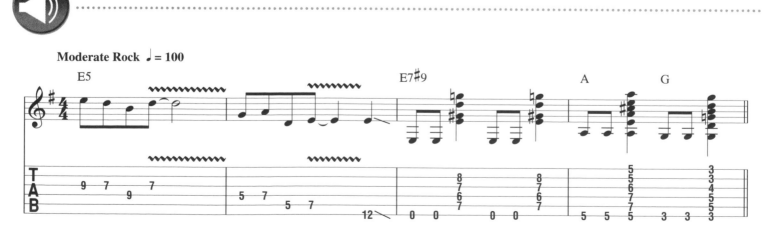

# JAMES HETFIELD

**James Alan Hetfield** (1963– ) was a Southern California outsider who started playing at age 14 and found solace in the music of Aerosmith. Answering an ad by Danish drummer Lars Ulrich led to them forming the thrash metal band Metallica in 1981. They recruited lead guitarist Dave Mustaine through another ad, and Hetfield sang and played rhythm guitar, as well as bass, on their first single. Bassist Cliff Burton joined for their debut, *Kill 'Em All* (1983). Nine studio albums, two live albums, five consecutive albums debuting at #1, and nine Grammy Awards later, Metallica live on with Kirk Hammett (having replaced Mustaine in 1983) and bassist Robert Trujillo (2003) on board. *Metallica* (1991) has sold over 22 million worldwide along with *Master of Puppets* (1986), their acknowledged classic.

## The Sound

Hetfield is a great riff man, as evidenced by "Enter Sandman" and many other tracks. His tone has bark and bite, but definition as well. He plays and endorses ESP guitars, including his signature Truckster model, along with a 1973 Les Paul and Electra Flying V copy through Marshall and Mesa Boogie amps. His effects are housed in a pedal board (offstage) and include a TC Electronic effects processor, Line 6 DM-4, and Mesa Boogie Custom Graphic Equalizer.

© Marty Temme

**Guitar:** 1973 Gibson Les Paul Custom, **ESP Explorer with EMG 81/ EMG 60 pickups**

**Amp:** Mesa Boogie Simul-Class 2:90

**Effects:** TC Electronic G-Major effects processor, Line 6 DM-4, Mesa Boogie Custom Graphic Equalizer, MXR Phase 100

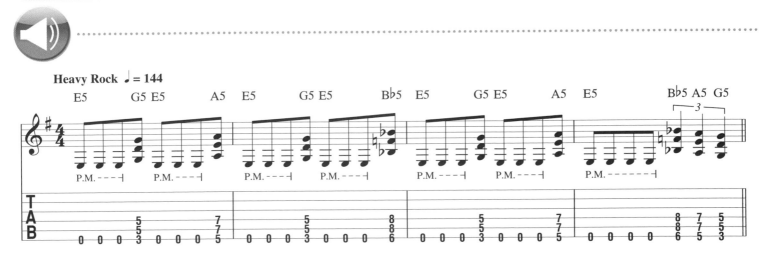

# ALLAN HOLDSWORTH

© Billy Tompkins / Retna

English virtuoso **Allan Holdsworth** (1946–2017) maintained artistic integrity, counter to commercial acceptance. His exceptionally fluid and scalar style was influenced by jazz saxophonists Charlie Parker and John Coltrane, as well as guitarists Django Reinhardt and Joe Pass. In the seventies, he played fusion jazz with Soft Machine, the Tony Williams Lifetime, and Bill Bruford. He became a bandleader in the eighties after being recognized by Eddie Van Halen. After relocating to Southern California, Holdsworth released a series of albums, including *Atavachron* (1986), which featured the SynthAxe. He opened a studio in 1992 and initiated a number of projects, including one with long-time collaborator and keyboardist, Gordon Beck. Since 2001, he only recorded one solo studio album, *Flat Tire: Music for a Non-Existent Movie*, while releasing live albums and a compilation.

## The Sound

Holdsworth was known for an extremely legato sound and experimented with a number of instruments to best achieve it. He tried Strats before settling on the SG in the seventies. An ES-335, Carvin guitars, and the Chapman Stick followed, along with the SynthAxe in the eighties. Vox AC30, Mesa Boogie, and Carvin amps were used with the Rocktron Intelliflex, Yamaha UD Stomp and Magicstomp effects boxes.

**Guitar:** SynthAxe, **Steinberger Signature model GL2TA-AH,** Carvin HF2 and HF2 Fatboy
**Amp:** Hughes & Kettner TriAmp Mark II and ZenTera, Yamaha DG80-112 modeling amp
**Effects:** Yamaha Magicstomp

# EARL HOOKER

**Earl Zebedee Hooker** (1929–1970) is considered to be the greatest Chicago blues guitarist and was a master of slide in standard tuning like Tampa Red and Robert Nighthawk. A Mississippian and cousin of John Lee Hooker, Earl was self-taught but generally avoided singing due to a speech impediment, a factor that would impact his career. By 1942, he was playing with Bo Diddley in Chicago and was greatly influenced by T-Bone Walker in both style and showmanship, as well as by Robert Nighthawk who mentored him on slide. He recorded from 1952 until his death from tuberculosis in 1970. Known more as a sideman, he left a legacy of classic instrumentals, including "Blues in D Natural" and "Blue Guitar," the latter of which Muddy Waters turned into "You Shook Me" in 1962.

## The Sound

Hooker was unique in his sound, as well as style, as he experimented more with guitars, amps, and effects than most other blues guitarists. He played a National, a Gibson SG, and two double-necks: a Danelectro 6/4 and a Gibson EDS-1275 6/12. Though he tried many other brands, Fender was his amp of choice, along with a wah pedal and a homemade tape system that allowed him to double track his guitar in performance.

© Michael Ochs Archive / Getty Images

**Guitar:** Circa-1959 Danelectro 6/4 double-neck, **1962–68 Gibson EDS-1275 6/12 double-neck**

**Amp:** Fender combo

**Effects:** Vox wah pedal, tape delay

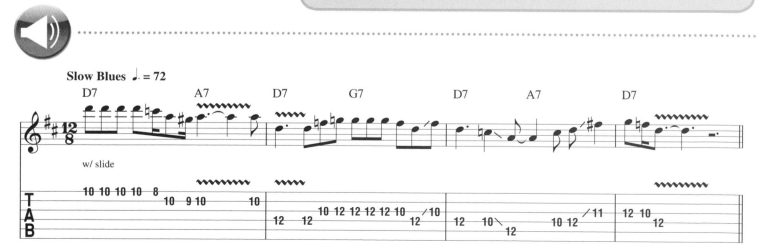

# JOHN LEE HOOKER

John Lee "The Boogie Man" Hooker (1917–2001) was one of a kind with the most primal and "primitive" Mississippi Delta blues. Derived from his stepfather, Will Moore, Hooker would use his pioneering style to change the face of blues after the recording of "Boogie Chillen" in 1948 in Detroit, which sold one million copies. He would go on to record over 100 albums of solo guitar and band blues with numerous classics like "Crawlin' King Snake," "Tupelo Blues," "I'm in the Mood," "House Rent Boogie," and "Boom Boom"; the latter made him a star in England in the early sixties and had a huge influence on British blues and rock bands. Hooker was inducted into the Rock and Roll Hall of Fame in 1991 and received a Lifetime Achievement Grammy in 2000.

## The Sound

The "Hook" went from over-amplified acoustic to hollowbody electrics with a tone that became progressively less distorted. He is first seen in 1949 with a Stella flat-top with a DeArmond pickup in the soundhole, followed by a 1952 Les Paul Goldtop (one of his few solidbodies), Guild M-75, Epiphone Sheraton (signature model in 2000), and Gibson ES-335, ES-345, and ES-330. Among others, he used Ampeg, Silvertone, and Fender amps.

© Photofest

> **Guitar:** 1960s Epiphone Sheraton, Gibson ES-330, Gibson ES-335
> **Amp:** Fender Concert, Fender Twin

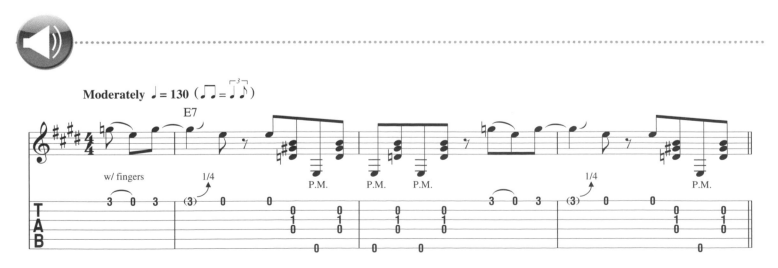

# TONY IOMMI

Many believe that heavy metal began with England's **Francis Anthony "Tony" Iommi** (1948– ). At 17, the southpaw guitarist lost the tips of his right hand's middle and ring fingers in a factory accident and made artificial replacements. Various heavy rock bands, including Jethro Tull (1968), preceded Iommi's arrival with Ozzy Osbourne (vocals), Terry "Geezer" Butler (bass), and Bill Ward (drums) in what would become Black Sabbath in 1969. The landmark *Paranoid* (1970) made their reputation, but breakups, reunions, and a lawsuit between Osbourne and Iommi over the use of the name would follow. In 2000, Iommi went solo, forming Heaven & Hell (2006) with Ward and singer Ronnie James Dio until Dio's death in 2010. Sabbath was inducted into the Rock and Roll Hall of Fame in 2006.

## The Sound

Iommi actually recorded parts of the first Sabbath album on a left-handed CBS-era Fender Strat and played two Les Pauls on *Paranoid*. However, a 1965 SG Special would become his main axe (played through Laney amps—they would later produce a signature model). Gibson would release a signature SG as well as a signature pickup. Iommi's "secret" effect was the Dallas Rangefinder Treble Booster (see Eric Clapton) that contributed to his classic metallic tone.

© Robert Knight

**Guitar:** 1965 Gibson SG Special ("Monkey") with John Birch custom single-coil pickups, Jaydee custom SG with 24-fret neck, **1997 Gibson Custom Shop Limited Edition Iommi Special SG prototype**

**Amp:** Laney Supergroup L.A. 100BL

**Effects:** Dallas Rangemaster Treble Booster, Tychobrahe Parapedal wah, Rotosound pedal

# ERIC JOHNSON

© PBS / Photofest

Texas native **Eric Johnson** (1954– ) is a respected instrumentalist equally known for his exceptional tone and fluid, tasteful playing. He began playing at 11 and was in a band by 15. In 1978, Johnson recorded *Seven Worlds* (released in 1994) with the Electromagnets and began playing on sessions. *Tones* (1986) garnered critical praise, while the platinum *Ah Via Musicom* (1990), featuring "Cliffs of Dover," won a Grammy for Best Rock Instrumental, as Johnson was regularly topping readers' polls. Six years elapsed for the perfectionist before a disappointing follow-up, but a collaboration with Joe Satriani and Steve Vai in G3 produced the platinum *G3 Live in Concert* (1997). Since then, Johnson has been involved in a number of projects, including albums for Favored Nations, two theatrical productions, and another tour with G3.

## The Sound

Johnson finesses a creamy, smooth tone from pre-CBS Strats, a Gibson ES-335, Custom Shop '59 Les Paul reissue, and Charvel Jackson. Martin released a signature MC-40 (2003), and Fender debuted a signature maple-neck Strat (2005) with a rosewood neck variation (2009). Johnson generally uses three amps ganged together: Marshall, Dumble, and Fender Twin, and a selection of effects including a TS-9 Tube Screamer, Electro-Harmonix Memory Man, TC Electronic 2290 delay, Echoplex, MXR flanger and digital delay.

**Guitar:** **1957 Fender Stratocaster**, 1990 Charvel Jackson
**Amp:** Dumble Steel String Singer, Marshall JTM45-100, Fender Twin Reverb
**Effects:** Ibanez TS-9 Tube Screamer, TC Electronic 2290 delay, Electro-Harmonix Memory Man

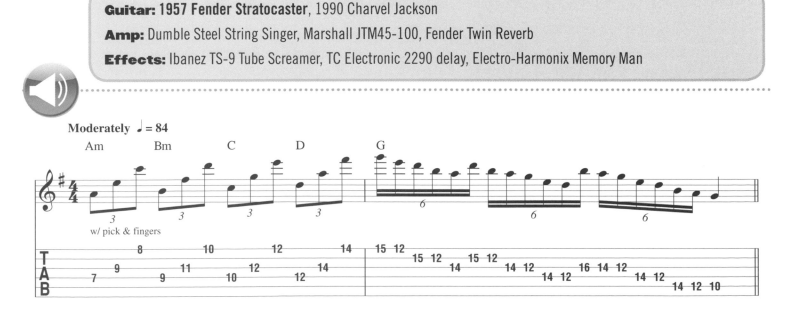

# LONNIE JOHNSON

B.B. King calls **Alonzo "Lonnie" Johnson** (1899–1970) the most influential guitarist of the twentieth century and the inventor of single-string soloing. He started out playing the violin and from 1925–32 turned out 130 singles, including jazz sides with both Louis Armstrong and Duke Ellington in 1927. In 1928–29, he waxed blues guitar duets with white jazz cat Eddie Lang—duets that are still astonishing today. Following the Great Depression, Johnson continued his pace and had an R&B hit in 1948 with "Tomorrow Night." Time passed him by in the fifties, and he became a janitor in a Philadelphia hotel before being rediscovered in 1959. He recorded a series of exceptional albums in the sixties before being struck by a car in Toronto in 1969; he died in 1970.

## The Sound

Johnson played acoustic guitars for the bulk of his career, including a custom-made Mexican 12-string early on, along with a Martin 00-21 and a 1942 Gibson J-100. During the sixties, he was seen playing solo electric guitar with a Kay thinline and a 1959–61 Gibson ES-330. He always favored a clean, unencumbered sound to accentuate his immaculate execution and swift, nimble phrasing.

© Michael Ochs Archive / Getty Images

**Guitar:** Custom 12-string acoustic with 10 strings, fifties Kay Value Leader, Gibson dot-neck ES-330

**Amp:** Fifties and sixties tube combos

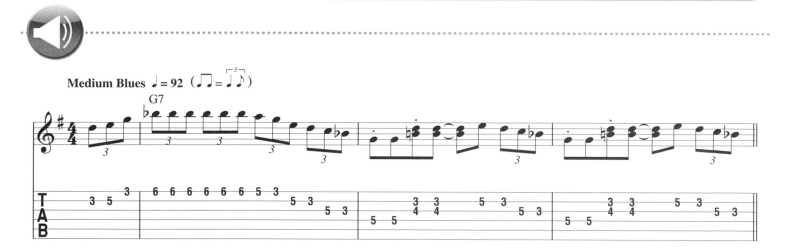

# ROBERT JOHNSON

Considered by many to be the greatest country blues guitarist, Mississippi guitarist **Robert Leroy Johnson** (1911–1938) learned directly from Ike Zinnerman and the records of Charley Patton, Lonnie Johnson, Son House, and others. He encouraged speculation about having received supernatural instrumental powers with songs like "Crossroads Blues," "Hellhound on My Trail," and "Me and the Devil Blues." Though more a synthesizer than an originator, his "Sweet Home Chicago," "(I Believe I'll) Dust My Broom," and "Ramblin' on My Mind" popularized the cut boogie pattern that would become prevalent in electric Chicago blues and early rock 'n' roll. The most mythic figure in the blues, he died (appropriately enough) after being poisoned by a jealous husband. In 1990, his box set of 29 songs sold more than 500,000 copies.

## The Sound

One of the few true virtuosos of pre-war country blues guitar, Johnson played fingerstyle with a plastic thumbpick that brought out the funky midrange of his small-body Gibson flat-top. Although an unconfirmed rumor, in the early seventies it was reported that Johnson had been seen playing an electric guitar in front of bass and drums just before his death in 1938.

**Guitar:** Late-twenties Gibson L-1, mid-thirties Kalamazoo

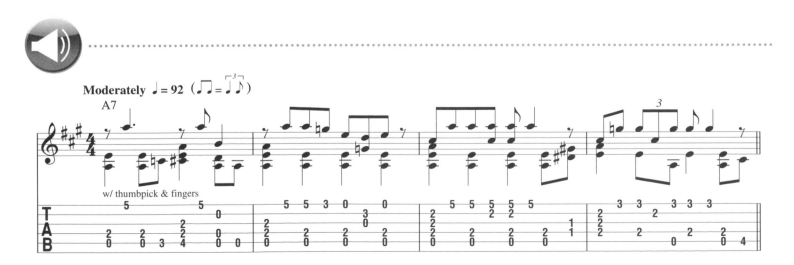

# JORMA KAUKONEN

© John Atashian / Retna Ltd.

Well known for his idiosyncratic psychedelic solos with the Jefferson Airplane (1965–72) on classics like "Somebody to Love" and "White Rabbit," Washington, D.C. guitarist **Jorma Kaukonen** (1940– ) played solo acoustic blues influenced by Rev. Gary Davis, and spent time with the likes of Janis Joplin in San Francisco in the early sixties. In 1969, he formed the acoustic Hot Tuna with Airplane bassist Jack Casady, and the two have recorded and performed acoustic and electric on and off ever since. Kaukonen and the Airplane were inducted into the Rock and Roll Hall of Fame in 1996. Since then, Kaukonen has gone on to become a respected country blues guitarist and educator. He released *Stars in My Crown* and *River of Time* in 2007 and 2009, respectively, showcasing his mastery of fingerstyle blues.

## The Sound

Originally a self-described "blues purist," Kaukonen had a straight electric guitar tone with a Gibson L-5 and ES-345 Stereo split between two Fender Twin Reverb amps. A Cry Baby wah and an Ampeg Scrambler fuzz box were his effects. He has also played a Gibson Nighthawk and Les Paul Goldtop, and in 2003 Epiphone released a Jorma Kaukonen Riviera Deluxe. His Piedmont fingerpicking style requires a plastic thumbpick and metal finger picks.

**Guitar:** Gibson ES-345, Epiphone Riviera, 1959 Gibson J-50, **Martin Jorma Kaukonen M-30**, Gibson Chet Atkins SST

**Amp:** Black-face Fender Twin Reverb, Carr Slant 6V, Fishman Loudbox

**Effects:** Cry Baby wah, Ampeg Scrambler, Aguilar DB 900 direct box

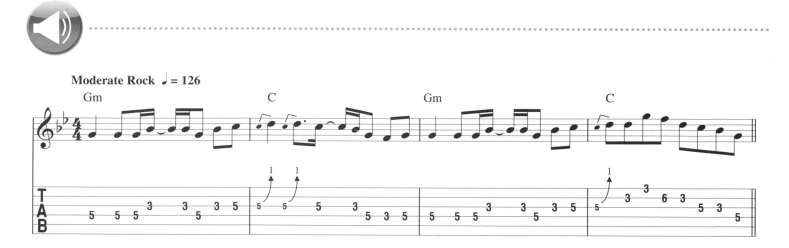

# ALBERT KING

© Fernando Aceves / Retna Ltd.

Joe Walsh crowed that, "Albert King could blow away most guitarists with his standby switch on," and it was hardly hyperbole. The "Velvet Bulldozer," born **Albert Nelson** (1923–1992) in Mississippi in 1932, is the most influential electric blues guitarist after B.B. King. Originally inspired by T-Bone Walker, he played drums behind Jimmy Reed before cutting his first singles in 1953. He moved to St. Louis and between 1959–63 recorded jump and slow blues produced by Ike Turner. Signing with Stax Records in Memphis in 1966 changed his career (and the course of the blues) following *Born Under a Bad Sign* (1967). He reached both black and white audiences until Stax went bust around 1976. Though bitter, King would record and play until a heart attack ended his life in 1992.

## The Sound

King plucked with his thumb on a right-handed 1958 Gibson Flying V named "Lucy," playing left-handed and upside down in his altered tuning of (low to high) B-E-B-E-G#-C# for a unique vocal style in phrasing and tone. He became famous with his solid-state Acoustic bass amp in the sixties, augmented by a Roland Jazz Chorus and occasionally an MXR Phase 90 in the seventies.

**Guitar:** 1958 Gibson Flying V, Erlewine copy of Flying V, **1988 Tom Holmes Flying V-type**

**Amp:** 1967 Acoustic 260 bass head with 261 cabinet with two 15" Altec speakers

**Effects:** MXR Phase 90

# B.B. KING

"The blues is a feeling," said Mississippian **Riley B. "B.B." King** (1925–2015). His modesty, which was only surpassed by his immense talent, prevented him from saying that the "feeling" must be translated into music in order to move people and that he accomplished that feat better than almost anyone else in the blues. He broke through to the R&B market with "Three O'Clock Blues" in 1951 and crossed over to the rock audience with "The Thrill Is Gone" in 1970. Perhaps second only to his idol Lonnie Johnson, King was clearly the most influential *electric* blues guitarist of the twentieth century. Virtually every picker who has bent and vibratoed a string owes a debt to the former "Beale Street Blues *Man*."

## The Sound

B.B. found that he could sustain notes in a vocal manner, beyond what a cranked amp offered, if he bent and vibratoed his strings while achieving a shimmering sound similar to the bottleneck style of country bluesmen like his cousin Bukka White. His first "Lucille" was a 1942 Gibson L-30, but his musical artillery has also included a 1950 ES-5N, 1957 ES-175D, 1959–60 ES-335, and 1966–67 ES-355TDC. Since 1980, he has played his signature Gibson "Lucille" model.

© Marty Temme

**Guitar:** Late-sixties Gibson ES-355, eighties Signature ES-355 Lucille
**Amp:** Late-sixties Fender Twin, Gibson Lab Series combo

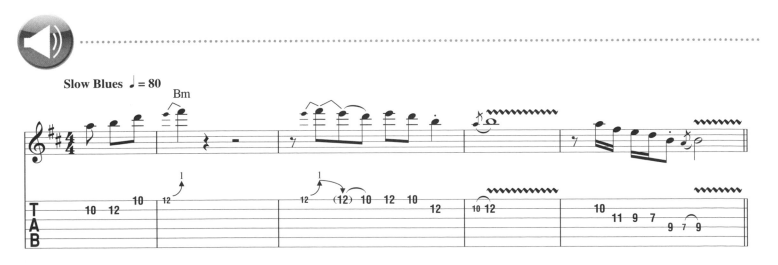

# FREDDIE KING

Texas-born guitarist **Frederick Christian** (1934–1976) was arguably the most talented of the "Three Kings of the Blues" with his virtuosic playing, singing, and songwriting. His mother taught him to play, and he took her maiden name. King moved to Chicago in 1952 and recorded his first singles in 1956 while jamming with Magic Sam, Otis Rush, and Buddy Guy. From 1960–66, he recorded an amazing number of classic instrumental and vocal tunes for King/Federal Records in Cincinnati, including "Hide Away," "San Ho-Zay," "The Stumble," and "Tore Down." He returned to Texas when Leon Russell on Shelter Records gave him a new lease on life in the seventies, as did King's friendship with Eric Clapton, which resulted in *Freddie King (1934–1976)*. He died at age 42 from bleeding ulcers.

## The Sound

As instructed by Jimmy Rogers in Chicago, King utilized a plastic thumbpick and metal index finger pick for a biting attack. Though he initially played a Gibson Les Paul Goldtop with P-90 pickups, after 1963 he would be most identified with a Gibson ES-345 and ES-355. For this studio work with King Records, he reportedly used a 50-watt Fender Twin. In the seventies, he "graduated" to a Fender Quad Reverb.

© Robert Knight

**Guitar:** 1956 Gibson Les Paul Goldtop, early sixties Gibson ES-345, late-sixties Gibson ES-355

**Amp:** 1957–60 Tweed Fender Twin, Dual Showman, Quad Reverb

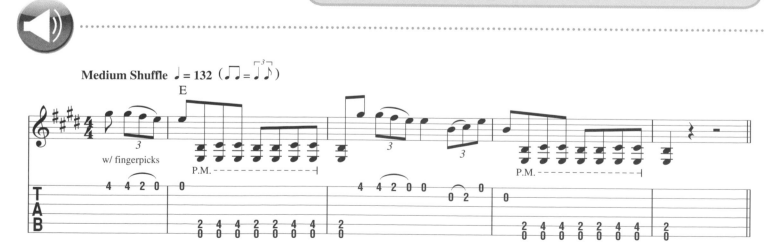

# MARK KNOPFLER

© David Plastik / Retna UK

Scottish English teacher **Mark Knopfler** (1949– ) formed Dire Straits in 1977. Their eponymous #2 debut hit (1978), driven by the #4 hit single "Sultans of Swing," led the way for rock music from the seventies to the eighties. Influenced by J.J. Cale and blues, folk, and country music, the band would release five more studio albums through to 1993, including the #1 Grammy-winning *Brothers in Arms* (1985), which featured the #1 Grammy-winning "Money for Nothing," "Walk of Life" (#6), and "So Far Away" (#19). In 1996, Knopfler began a solo career with *Golden Heart* while continuing to produce, play on soundtracks, and guest with other artists. In 2003, he was involved in a serious motorcycle accident in London but recovered and rebounded with his latest release, *Get Lucky* (2009).

## The Sound

The silvery, singing tone of a lightly overdriven vintage Strat typifies the classic Knopfler sound, and as a result, Fender released a signature red Strat in 2007. Outside of the heavy Les Paul distortion on "Money for Nothing," his sound has been relatively refined. Early on, Knopfler's main amp was a brown tolex Fender Vibrolux, but he has also employed a variety of other Fender, Marshall, Music Man, Roland, Mesa Boogie, and Soldano amps.

**Guitar:** 1961, 1961–62, and 1954 Fender Stratocasters, Pensa-Suhr R Custom, 1958, 1959, and 1984 Gibson Les Paul Standards, **Schecter Strat-type**, 1937 National Style O

**Amp:** Early sixties Fender Vibrolux, silver-face Fender Twin Reverb, Music Man HD-130

**Effects:** Dan Armstrong Orange Squeezer, Aphex Exciter, Roland Chorus, Morley volume pedal, Ernie Ball volume pedal, MXR analog delay

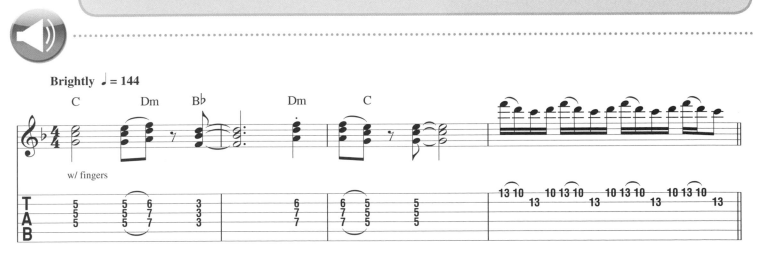

# LEO KOTTKE

© Andrew Lepley

Georgia-born **Leo Kottke** (1945– ) moved to the Midwest after being discharged from the Naval Reserve following ear damage. Using his advanced fingerstyle chops that had been developing since discovering Mississippi John Hurt at age 11, he played the Minneapolis-St. Paul folk scene and recorded the live *12-String Blues* in 1969. Signing with John Fahey's Takoma label resulted in the land-mark instrumental *6- and 12-String Guitar* (1969) that boasted his unparalleled virtuosity. Heading into the seventies, he was encouraged to sing, and he reluctantly unleashed his deadpan baritone and warped sense of humor. A serious bout with right-hand tendonitis in the eighties forced him to alter his attack, and he studied classical and jazz tech-nique. His last release was *Sixty-Six Steps* (2005) with bassist Mike Gordon (Phish).

## The Sound

Kottke plays acoustic fingerstyle and slide in open G, D, and standard tuning (though often tuned down in pitch two whole steps) and made his mark with the 12-string guitar. He played custom Bozo Podu-navac guitars in the seventies, one of which had a 34-inch scale to accommodate his detuning, and he has also picked Gibson and Martin guitars. In 1990, Taylor introduced a signature 12-string followed by a 6-string flat-top in 1997.

**Guitar:** Early-seventies Bozo Podunavac 12-string, **Taylor LKSM Signature 12-string and 6-string models**

# EDDIE LANG

The "Father of Jazz Guitar," virtuoso **Eddie Lang** (1902–1933) was born Salvatore Massaro in Philadelphia. He studied violin but switched to guitar 11 years later and was professionally playing both (along with the banjo) by the twenties. A master of chordal accompaniment and single-note soloing, he enjoyed great success and influence as an accompanist and soloist with Bix Beiderbecke, Paul Whiteman—with whom he appeared in *King of Jazz*—and Bing Crosby. His sensational blues duets with Lonnie Johnson in 1928–29 (under the name Blind Willie Dunn, due to racial restrictions) were the first recorded blues duets. In 1930, he played on the original recording of "Georgia on My Mind" with Beiderbecke and Joe Venuti. Lang died tragically following a botched tonsillectomy.

## The Sound

Lang was one of the first to play a Gibson L-5 following its debut in 1922, though he first played an L-4 that originally had an oval soundhole rather than f-holes. The greater projection and stronger midrange and upper register of the archtop guitar allowed him to substantially expand his range with chords and scales.

**Guitar:** 1929 Gibson L-5

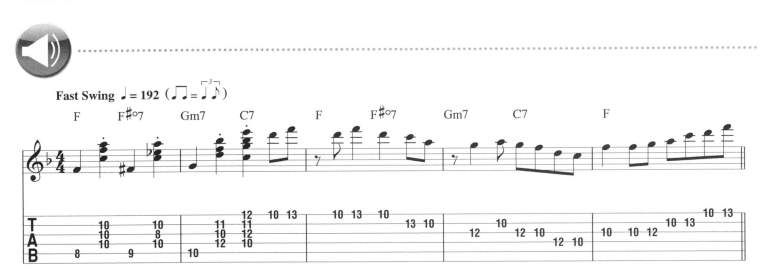

# ALBERT LEE

Ace British chicken picker **Albert Lee** (1943– ) has been a highly sought after sideman. Starting out on the piano, he was drawn to the guitar in the mid fifties when he heard the rock 'n' roll of Jerry Lee Lewis, Buddy Holly, and then the advanced hot country guitar of Jimmy Bryant, Cliff Gallup, and James Burton. By age 16, he was a session man, playing in a number of top R&B outfits before joining the progressive country band Heads, Hands & Feet where he first cut "Country Boy." Moving to Los Angeles in 1974 led to his taking Burton's place with Emmy Lou Harris, and he backed Eric Clapton from 1978–83. In 2003, he received a Grammy for "Foggy Mountain Breakdown" from *Earl Scruggs and Friends*.

## The Sound

An honored member of the great Tele pickers club, Lee plays clean with a clearer sound than most. He currently has 1952, 1953, and 1960 models, along with a circa-1960 Gibson Les Paul Custom given to him by Eric Clapton (via Delaney and Bonnie). In addition, Don Everly gave him a Gibson J-200. Lee uses Music Man, Fender, and Rivera amps, and delay is an integral part of his sound.

© Phil Dent

**Guitar:** 1953 Fender Telecaster, **late-seventies bound-top Tele-type**, Ernie Ball Music Man 90 Signature model with B-Bender

**Amp:** Music Man HD-130 2x10 and 4x10, Fender Tone Master

**Effects:** Korg A-3 digital delay processor

# YNGWIE MALMSTEEN

Born in Sweden as **Lars Johan Yngwie Lannerback** (1963– ), he epitomized shredding in the eighties. Originally inspired by Jimi Hendrix and Ritchie Blackmore at age ten, he became obsessed with classical music, especially Paganini, for inspiration to develop his devastating chops. Mike Varney heard his demo and invited him to the U.S. in 1981 to join Steeler. After one album, Malmsteen bolted to Alcatrazz before forming Rising Force, releasing an eponymous album (#60) in 1984 that "electrified" guitarists. *Marching Out* (#54 in 1985) and *Trilogy* (#44 in 1986) followed before his life began to unravel. In 1987, a serious car accident forced him to regain the use of his right hand while weathering numerous setbacks and scandals. He remains popular in Asia, and his last release was *Instru-Mental* (2007).

## The Sound

Malmsteen is a loyal Strat slinger and has mainly played his iconic 1972 model like his idol Ritchie Blackmore (with a scalloped fingerboard—a feature that both players believe facilitates technique). Fender released a signature model in 1988, the second such tribute (after Eric Clapton). True to his persona, Malmsteen has gone for overkill with his amps, using as many as 24 Marshall Mark II 50-watt heads and 4x12 cabinets in the eighties.

© Marty Temme

**Guitar:** 1972 Fender Stratocaster ("The Duck"), **Signature Fender Stratocaster**

**Amp:** 1971 Marshall Mark II head with 4x12 cabinet

**Effects:** Korg DL8000R Stereo and Mono delays, TC Electronic G-Force chorus/pitch shift, DOD Overdrive Preamp 250, Boss OC-2 Octave, NS-2 Noise Suppressor, and BF-2 Flanger, Ibanez TS-9 Tube Screamer

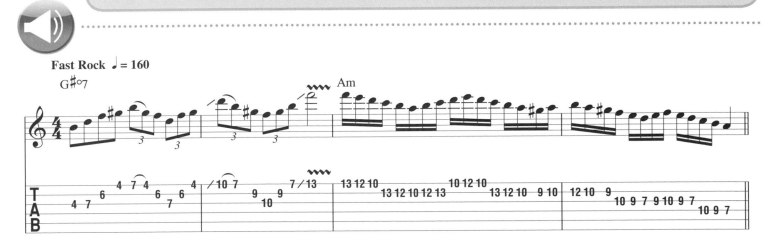

# BRIAN MAY

© Marty Temme

**Brian Harold May** (1947– ) was the instantly-recognizable instrumental voice in Queen. He played ukulele and piano before receiving a guitar at age seven. He and his father then built a guitar together that would become known as the iconic "Red Special." Influenced by Hank Marvin, Scotty Moore, and Buddy Holly, May convened the instrumental band 1984 in the mid sixties before forming Smile, which would evolve into Queen with the addition of singer Freddie Mercury. From 1973 until Mercury's death in 1991, the band scored 18 #1 albums and 18 #1 singles and was inducted into the Rock and Roll Hall of Fame in 2001. May released the EP *Star Fleet Project* in 1983 followed by *Back to the Light* (1993) and *Another World* (1998).

## The Sound

May's sound consists of compressed sustain, multi-tracked harmonies, and an English sixpence for a plectrum. The "Red Special" contains Burns Tri-Sonic pickups wired in series for natural overdrive. A signature model was released by Guild in 1984 with DiMarzio pickups, and another model was released in 1993 with Seymour Duncan pickups. In concert, he plays a stack of 12(!) Vox AC30 amps, and in the studio, May uses a small transistor amp built by Queen bassist John Deacon.

**Guitar:** Original "Red Special," 1984 Guild BHM1, and 1993 signature model

**Amp:** Vox AC30, custom "Deacy" amp reproduced by Vox as the Brian May Special

**Effects:** Dallas Rangemaster treble booster, Pete Cornish treble booster, Greg Fryer treble booster, Foxx Foot Phaser, Two Echoplexes

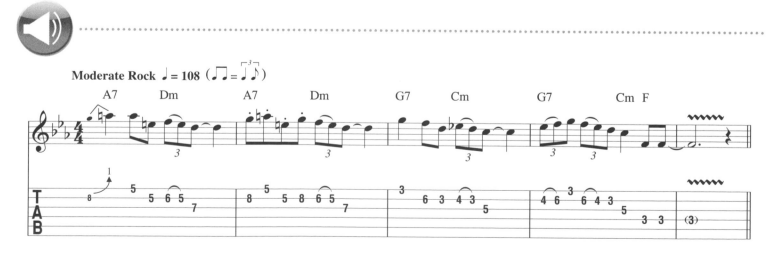

# ROGER McGUINN

Chicago native **James Joseph "Roger" McGuinn III** (1942– ) would change the face of rock with his electric 12-string guitar. The young folkie backed the Limelighters, the Chad Mitchell Trio, Bobby Darin, and Judy Collins before forming the Byrds in L.A. in 1964 with David Crosby, Gene Clark, Chris Hillman, and Michael Clarke. Following their landmark cover of Bob Dylan's "Mr. Tambourine Man" and the folk staple "Turn! Turn! Turn!" (both #1 in 1965), they would go on to great success as folk rock pioneers before the constant internal tension ended the band's run in 1973 after their landmark country rock classic *Sweetheart of the Rodeo* (1968). Three partial reunions occurred in 1977, 1981, and 1989 while McGuinn pursued various solo projects. The Byrds were inducted into the Rock and Roll Hall of Fame in 1991.

## The Sound

McGuinn was playing acoustic 12-string guitars in 1957 and was inspired to buy a Rickenbacker electric 12-string after seeing George Harrison with one in *A Hard Day's Night.* The addition of compression and an altered tuning helped create the Byrds' signature sound; equally important, he plugged directly into the board in the studio. McGuinn also played a Gretsch Country Gentleman and used Fender Dual Showman amps onstage.

© Chris Daniels / Retna Ltd.

**Guitar:** 1965 Rickenbacker 360/12 12-string, 1965 Gretsch Country Gentleman, **signature Rickenbacker 370/12/RM 12-string**, signature Martin D12-42RM, signature Martin HD-7

**Amp:** Epiphone Ensign, Fender Dual Showman

**Effects:** Vox Treble Booster, Janglebox compressor

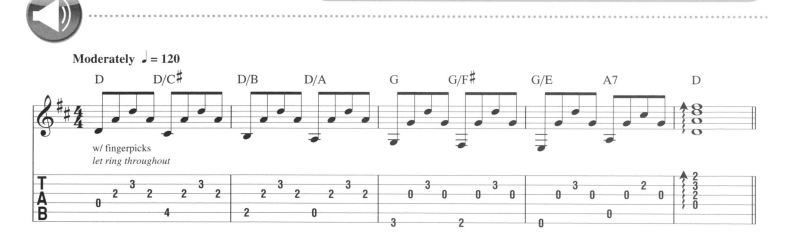

# JOHN McLAUGHLIN

British jazz and fusion virtuoso **John McLaughlin** (1942– ) started playing at age 11 after being inspired by blues and swing music. He released his debut album, *Extrapolation*, in 1969. After moving to New York City, he joined the Tony Williams Lifetime fusion band and then played with Miles Davis on the landmark albums *In a Silent Way* (1969) and *Bitches Brew* (1970). Combining spirituality with acoustic and Eastern music, McLaughlin recorded *My Goals Beyond* (1970) and *Devotion* (1970) before assembling the fusion powerhouse Mahavishnu Orchestra in 1971 for *The Inner Mounting Flame* (1971), *Birds of Fire* (1972), and *Visions of the Emerald Beyond* (1974). A collaboration with Carlos Santana in 1972 was followed by his band Shakti, which explored acoustic jazz and Indian music. His latest album, *To the One*, was released in 2010.

© Marty Temme

## The Sound

While McLaughlin has moved between electric and acoustic guitars throughout his long career, his picking has always been stupendously brisk and clean. He played a Gibson Hummingbird with a pickup as well as a Fender Mustang through to Miles Davis, followed by a Les Paul, a Gibson double-neck guitar, a custom double-neck guitar ("Double Rainbow"), a custom acoustic guitar with sympathetic strings, and MIDI guitars. Marshall and Mesa Boogie amps and basic effects pedals have served his sound requirements.

**Guitar:** Gibson Hummingbird, 1958 Gibson Les Paul Custom, 1964 Gibson L4CECC, 1971 Gibson EDS-1275 double-neck 6/12, **Rex Bogue custom double-neck**, Gibson Les Paul Deluxe, Abraham Wechter custom, Gibson J-200 "Shakti" acoustic, Godin MIDI

**Amp:** 100-watt Marshall half stack, Mesa Boogie Mark I

**Effects:** DeArmond volume pedal, Maestro PS-1, Dunlop Cry Baby wah

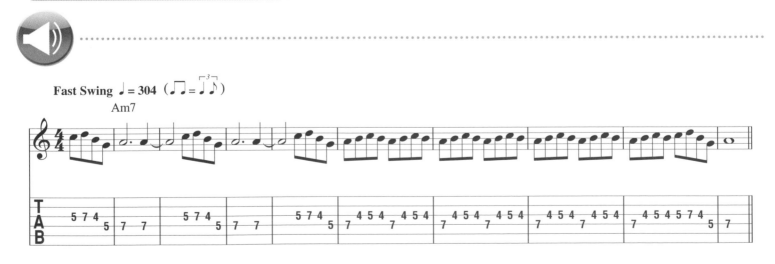

# PAT METHENY

**Patrick Bruce Metheny** (1954– ) brought accessible jazz to a rock audience in the eighties. Inspired by Wes Montgomery, he started playing at age 13 and was so advanced as a teenager that he taught at the University of Miami and Berklee School of Music. In 1974, he recorded with pianist Paul Bley and bassist Jaco Pastorius, followed by a stint with Gary Burton before going out on his own in 1978 with *Bright Size Life* (#28). *American Garage* (1980), which featured keyboardist Lyle Mays, hit #1. His ongoing career as a leader and sideman (with three gold records and 20 Grammy Awards) has featured many stylistic twists with notable jazz artists such as Sonny Rollins, Herbie Hancock, and Ornette Coleman. *What It's All About*, his latest release, appeared in 2011.

## The Sound

Though long identified with the natural, amplified, acoustic sound of his venerable Gibson ES-175, Metheny has also played a 12-string electric as well as the Roland GR-300 guitar synthesizer. He has also played a triple-neck, 42-string custom Pikasso 1 harp guitar on a number of albums. A solid state Acoustic was his only amp for 20 years, before he changed to a Digitech preamp combined with two delay pedals.

© Marty Temme

**Guitar:** 1958 Gibson ES-175D, **Ibanez PM100 Signature**, Linda Manzer Pikasso

**Amp:** Acoustic 134, Digitech 2101 DSP preamp

**Effects:** Two Lexicon Prime-Time digital delay pedals

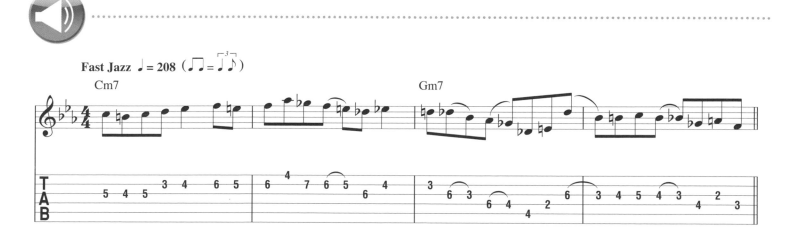

# WES MONTGOMERY

The most accomplished successor to Charlie Christian, **John Leslie "Wes" Montgomery** (1925–1968) began playing at the age of 18. He used his thumb instead of a pick, reportedly to practice quietly and not disturb others. After a tour with Lionel Hampton (1948–50) he labored in obscurity in Indianapolis clubs throughout the fifties with his brothers Monk and Buddy while working a day gig. *The Incredible Jazz Guitar of Wes Montgomery* (1960) was a landmark of modern post-bop guitar. However, in 1967, tired of struggling financially, he began playing simplified, octave-laden melodies on pop songs for A&M Records, and the substantial commercial results were unprecedented. Tragically, at the height of his newfound fame, Montgomery died from a heart attack at age 43.

## The Sound

Montgomery created a fat, rich tone with his thumb. He borrowed a Gibson ES-175 and tweed Fender Deluxe from Kenny Burrell for his first recordings. He later acquired a Gibson L-5, one of three similar models with a pickup in the neck position. The manufacturer would make three custom guitars for him with a reversed pickup like the signature model they introduced in 1993. A Fender black-face Super Reverb, 1965 Standel Custom XV, and a black-face Fender Twin Reverb provided amplification.

**Guitar:** 1961 Gibson L-5
**Amp:** Pre-CBS Fender Super Reverb

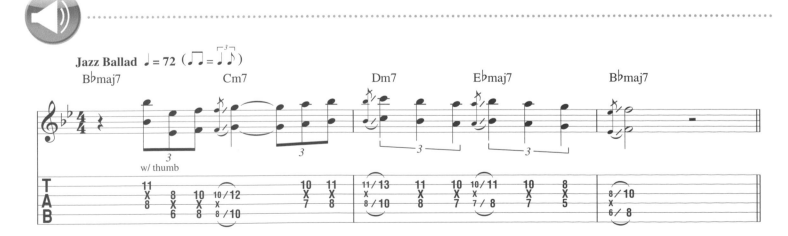

# SCOTTY MOORE

Tennessean **Winfield Scott "Scotty" Moore III** (1931–2016) will forever be linked with Elvis Presley and praised as a pioneer of rock 'n' roll guitar. After serving in the Navy from 1948–52, Moore moved to Memphis to lead the Starlight Wranglers where he met upright bassist Bill Black. In 1954, they were drafted by Sun Records honcho Sam Phillips to back a young Elvis, and rock was "born." Moore played electric guitar behind the King and also helped guide his career until 1958, but he was never adequately compensated for this work as promised. He appeared on the famous Presley television "Comeback Special" in 1968 and released *The Guitar That Changed the World* (1964) and *All the King's Men* (1997) featuring Keith Richards, Jeff Beck, Levon Helm, and Ron Wood.

## The Sound

Like rock 'n' roll itself, Moore's playing combined aspects of blues, country, and even jazz. He played a 1952 Fender Esquire when he got out of the Navy. However, as a fan of Chet Atkins, he played with a thumbpick and fingers on Gibson hollowbody guitars through a custom Ray Butts amp with built-in slap-back tape delay. He also used Elvis' various Martin D-18 flat-top guitars on occasion.

© Steve Bonner

**Guitar:** 1953 Gibson ES-295, 1954 Gibson L-5 CESN, **1956 Gibson Super 400 CESN**, 1963 Gibson Super 400 CES

**Amp:** 1952 Fender Deluxe, fifties Ray Butts 25-watt EchoSonic with two 50-watt booster cabinets

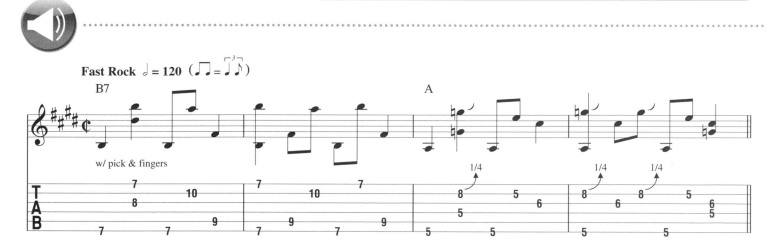

# JIMMY PAGE

British star **James Patrick Page** (1944– ) is one of the greatest innovators and improvisers in rock. Self-taught from age 12 and influenced by Scotty Moore and James Burton, "Pagey" became a top session guitarist before replacing bassist Paul Samwell-Smith in the Yardbirds in 1966, prior to joining Jeff Beck as co-lead guitarist. When Beck left, Page remained in the Yardbirds until 1968 when he formed Led Zeppelin. Following their breakup in 1980 after the death of drummer John Bonham, Page played in the Firm with Paul Rodgers, recorded with Plant, and reunited with Zep for brief reunions, including one in 2007 with John Bonham's son Jason on drums. Led Zeppelin had six #1 albums, sold more than 200 million records, and was inducted into the Rock and Roll Hall of Fame in 1995.

## The Sound

Page is best known for his iconic Les Paul burst, but played a Fender Telecaster (given to him by Jeff Beck) on the solo for "Stairway to Heaven" and the first Led Zeppelin album. The ultimate "tonemeister," he often achieved his classic tone by plugging straight into an amp with minimal effects. Page also is an excellent fingerstyle guitarist; he plays a Martin D-18, a Gibson Everly Brothers model, and records with a Gibson J-200.

© Photofest

**Guitar:** 1960 Gibson Les Paul Custom, 1958 Fender Telecaster, **1959 Gibson Les Paul Standard ("Number One")**, 1959 Gibson Les Paul Standard (modified), Fender Electric XII, Gibson EDS-1275 double-neck 6/12, 1960 Danelectro 3021

**Amp:** 1958–59 Supro 1690TN Coronado (modified), Marshall SLP-1959 100-watt stack

**Effects:** Maestro FZ-1 Fuzztone, Sola Sound Tonebender Mark II, Vox wah

# BRAD PAISLEY

© Robert Knight

**Bradley Douglas Paisley** (1972– ) has utilized his bluegrass, rock, and West Virginia roots to become a virtuosic country mega-star. At eight, his grandfather supplied him with a guitar and a love of Merle Travis, Chet Atkins, and Les Paul. By age ten, he was performing in public and was a regular on "Jamboree USA" from 1984–90. He went to college 1993–95 on an ASCAP scholarship, which led to a songwriting deal with EMI. The platinum *Who Needs Pictures* (#13 in 2000) was the first of seven albums down to *American Saturday Night* (#2 in 2010) that have all gone gold or better. So far, he has had 15 #1 singles and won three Grammys, 13 Academy of Country Music Awards, and 13 Country Music Association Awards.

## The Sound

Gear is far more important to Paisley than most of his black cowboy-hatted peers as he unapologetically strives for distortion and sustain. Besides the obligatory Fender Telecaster, including the obvious late-sixties paisley-finish model, he also plays Crook Tele-style guitars fitted with string benders. Paisley has played a variety of Fenders, along with Vox AC30, Trainwreck, and Dr. Z amps. His long list of effects includes various delay, echo, and distortion boxes.

---

**Guitar:** 1968 paisley-finish Fender Telecaster ("Old Pink"), Crook custom Tele-style with McVay G-bender

**Amp:** Dr. Z Stingray heads with cabinets containing Weber and Celestion speakers, Vox AC30

**Effects:** Line 6 Echo Pro Delay, Modulation Pro and Filter Pro, Diamond compressor, Valve Train Amplification tube reverb, Fulltone Tube Tape Echo, Xotic Effects RC and AC Boosters, Keeley Modified Baked TS-9, Boss DD-2 Digital Delay, Zendrive, Aqua Puss Analog Delay

Country Rock ♩ = 130

w/ pick & fingers

# JOE PASS

© Lebrecht Music and Arts Photo Library / Alamy

Jazz master and New Jersey native **Joseph Anthony Jacobi Passalacqua** (1929–1994) was originally inspired by Gene Autry, but went on to be called the "President of Bebop." By age 14, he was out on the road, but he fell into the pitfalls of drug addiction in the fifties and spent two years in Synanon in California. Following rehab, he began recording a series of classic albums in the early sixties and went on to become a sideman for a long list of luminaries, including Frank Sinatra, Sarah Vaughan, and Joe Williams. Duo work with Herb Ellis, Ella Fitzgerald, and as a member of the Oscar Peterson Trio, as well as his landmark solo *Virtuoso* albums in the seventies, are a lasting testament to his greatness. Pass died from liver cancer at the all-too-young age of 65.

## The Sound

A classic, clean, vibrant, hollowbody archtop tone exemplifies the warm sound of Pass. He was known to say that he would play unamplified if he could be heard. For decades he was identified with the Gibson ES-175. In 1980, Ibanez brought out a signature JP20 model and Epiphone released a signature Emperor in 1994. Pass would generally play whatever amps were available in the studio before settling on the Polytone Brute.

**Guitar:** 1962 Gibson ES-175D, Ibanez JP20, Epiphone Joe Pass Emperor II, custom D'Aquisto

**Amp:** Polytone Mini-Brute

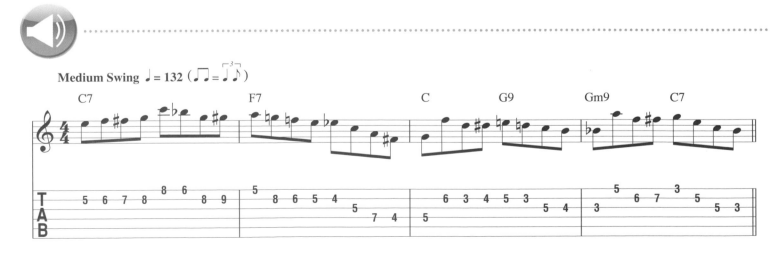

# LES PAUL

Along with Leo Fender, **Lester William "Les Paul" Polsfuss** (1915–2009) revolutionized both the electric guitar and audio recording. He first recorded under the pseudonym "Rhubarb Red" in Chicago in 1936. Influenced by Django Reinhardt, he formed the Les Paul Trio and relocated to New York City in 1939. Dissatisfied with the current amplified guitars of the 1930s, he experimented with a solidbody guitar. Moving to Hollywood resulted in a friendship with Bing Crosby who encouraged his research with multi-track recording. Following Fender's example, Gibson produced the first Les Paul model guitar in 1952 while Les and his wife, Mary Ford, went on to great success as recording and TV stars during the 1950s. Paul was inducted into the Rock and Roll Hall of Fame in 1988 and died of pneumonia at age 94.

## The Sound

Paul had a clean, warm tone before the debut of his world famous signature guitar. He would then tinker tirelessly to develop an even cleaner sound. Paul developed the Professional and Personal guitars in 1969 and the Recording model in 1972 (with low impedance and [distortion-free] pickups) while rock and blues guitarists drove their "Lesters" hard into distortion. He likely played Gibson amps in the fifties, including the various Les Paul models.

© Pictorial Press Ltd / Alamy

**Guitar:** 1940 Epiphone "Log," **1952 Gibson Les Paul Goldtop**, 1954 Gibson Les Paul Custom

**Amp:** Gibson GA-40

**Effects:** Tape delay, tape phasing

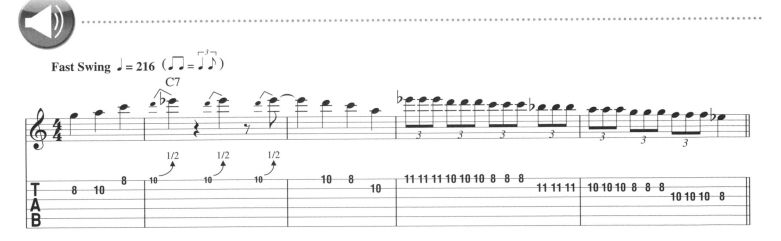

# JOE PERRY

Massachusetts-born guitarist **Anthony Joseph Perry** (1950– ) is the lead guitarist in Aerosmith. In 1970, he formed the Boston band with Tom Hamilton, Steven Tyler, and Joey Kramer; Brad Whitford was added in 1971. Known as "America's Rolling Stones" and the best-selling American band of all time, their 1973 self-titled recording debut contained "Dream On" while *Toys in the Attic* (#11 in 1975) broke them with "Walk This Way" (#10). Aerosmith has won four singles Grammys and scored two #1 albums with *Get a Grip* (1993) and *Nine Lives* (1997). Perry left from 1979–84 to pursue the Joe Perry Project and he and Tyler have battled substance abuse through the years. Aerosmith was inducted into the Rock and Roll Hall of Fame in 2001.

## The Sound

Perry was substantially influenced by Jeff Beck, Peter Green, and Jimmy Page, and hence, has mainly been a Les Paul man with a bright, overdriven tone. With a collection of 600 (!) guitars, he has many Pauls, including a signature Joe Perry Boneyard model. He also plays a Gibson ES-335, various Strats and Teles, and a newer Dan Armstrong plexiglass guitar. Marshall and Fender amps and an array of effects complete his big sound.

© Marty Temme

**Guitar:** 1958 Gibson Les Paul Standard, **mid-seventies Gibson Les Paul Custom**, Signature Gibson Joe Perry Boneyard Les Paul, seventies B.C. Rich Bich, mid-seventies left-handed Fender Stratocaster

**Amp:** 1970 Marshall Super Lead, 1964 Marshall 8x10, 1969 Marshall Super Bass head, 1963 Fender Vibroverb, 1973 Fender Dual Showman Reverb with 2x15 cabinet

**Effects:** DigiTech whammy pedal, Fulltone Tube Tape Echo, Dunlop DCR-1S Rackmount wah, Line 6 DL-4 Delay Modeler, Klon Centaur, Electro-Harmonix Deluxe Memory Man and POG

# JOHN PETRUCCI

© Marty Temme

Long Island's **John Petrucci** (1967– ) is a progressive metal guitar hero who is known for his work with Dream Theater. Influenced by Yngwie Malmsteen, Allan Holdsworth, and Steve Morse, he began playing at age 12. Petrucci attended the Berklee School of Music where he met John Myung (bass) and Mike Portnoy (drums) in 1985, the rhythm section of Majesty and then Dream Theater. *When Dream and Day Unite* (1989) was followed by their most successful *Images and Words* (1992); to date, nine others have followed. Even though Petrucci was recognized as a technical monster, personnel changes hampered the band, and he eventually found himself at the G3 gig six times with Steve Vai and Joe Satriani. He wrote a popular column for *Guitar World,* produced an instructional video, and recorded two tracks for a Sega Saturn video game.

## The Sound

Like most of his contemporaries, Petrucci has gone through extensive gear changes to achieve his classic metal tone of long, compressed sustain and smooth distortion in the upper register. He has enjoyed signature guitars from Ibanez, Ernie Ball, and especially the Music Man John Petrucci BFR models (with DiMarzio pickups) connected to a variety of Mesa Boogie amps and enhanced with an array of effects including TC Electronic, Boss, and MXR pedals.

**Guitar:** Ernie Ball EB/MM John Petrucci BFR, Music Man John Petrucci BFR baritone, Music Man John Petrucci Stealth 7-string

**Amp:** Mesa Boogie Mark V with Rectifier 4x12 cabinet

**Effects:** Keeley-modified TS-9 Tube Screamer, Dunlop DSR-25R rack wah, TC Electronic C400XL compressor/gate, Eventide H7600 Harmonizer

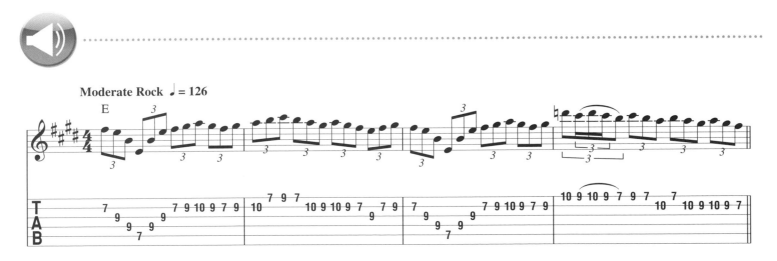

# JERRY REED

© Photofest

**Jerry Reed Hubbard** (1937–2008), the "Guitar Man" from Georgia, first recorded at age 18 but was not recognized until Gene Vincent covered his "Crazy Legs" in 1958. He moved to Nashville in 1961 as a songwriter, and his music was covered by Elvis while hitting the charts with "Guitar Man" (1967). "Amos Moses" (1970) was a crossover hit (#8), and he teamed up with Chet Atkins and appeared on TV. The title track from his first album, "When You're Hot, You're Hot" (1971) went #1 in the country genre. In the seventies, he became a movie actor with his buddy, Burt Reynolds, while advancing his recording career. Reed won three Grammys, including Best Country Instrumental Performance for *Sneakin' Around* (1992) with Atkins. He died of emphysema at age 71.

## The Sound

Reed was a "good ole' boy" with a twangy, hybrid-picking style inspired by Merle Travis and Chet Atkins, as evidenced on "The Claw" (1967), his signature instrumental. He played a classic Gretsch 6120 in the fifties, but made a radical change to a nylon-string Guild and then a nylon-string Baldwin with a pickup. In the late seventies, he tried his hand with a Tele-inspired Peavey T-60 through Peavey amps.

**Guitar:** Fifties Gretsch 6120, **sixties Guild nylon-string classical**, sixties Baldwin nylon-string with Prismatone piezo pickup, Peavey T-60

**Amp:** Peavey Session 400

# DJANGO REINHARDT

With spectacular technique and a gift for melody, the Belgian gypsy, **Jean "Django" Reinhardt** (1910–1953), is perhaps the greatest jazz guitarist of all time. He played violin, banjo, and guitar as a child while living in gypsy caravans outside of Paris. At age 18, his left hand was severely burned in a fire and his ring and pinky fingers became partially paralyzed, necessitating unorthodox fingerings. Discovering American jazz through Louis Armstrong and Duke Ellington, he formed the Quintet of the Hot Club of Paris in 1934 with violinist Stephane Grappelli, producing classics like "Minor Swing," "Djangology," and "Nuages," among many others, including later experiments with bebop. In 1946, he toured the U.S., met Les Paul, and played and recorded with Ellington. Reinhardt died tragically from a brain hemorrhage at age 43.

## The Sound

Originally influenced by gypsy musicians, Reinhardt added jazz to his traditional music background in 1929–33, developing a unique style that featured dazzling, two-finger runs and unusual chord voicings. He favored the iconic acoustic Selmer Maccaferri, first with the D-shaped soundhole and then a round-hole model after 1939. He also dabbled with the electric guitar, including a new Gibson ES-300, an L-5, and later, the Maccaferri with a pickup.

© GAB Archive / Redferns / Getty Images

**Guitar:** 1933 Selmer Maccaferri with D soundhole, 1939 Maccaferri with round soundhole, 1945 Gibson ES-300, 1946 Gibson L-5

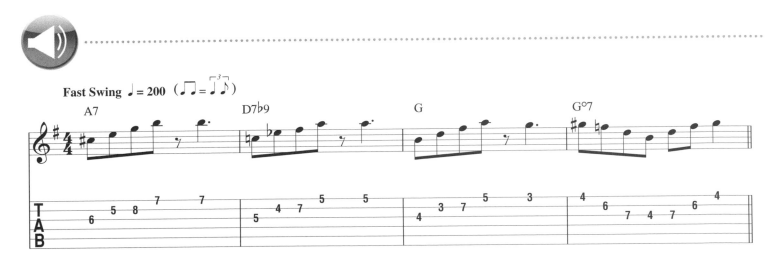

# RANDY RHOADS

A beloved guitar hero, **Randall William Rhoads** (1956–1982) came from a musical California family and was playing at age ten. Initially drawn to Mountain, Led Zeppelin, and Alice Cooper, he evolved beyond Eddie Van Halen's influence and incorporated classical music into his playing. He formed Quiet Riot in 1972 before Ozzy Osbourne drafted him in 1979. His playing on Ozzy's debut solo album *Blizzard of Ozz* (#21 in 1980) was a revelation, containing the metal classic "Crazy Train" (#9). *Diary of a Madman* (#16 in 1981) followed, and the accolades poured. However, he considered taking a break from rock to study classical guitar at UCLA, but a criminally-irresponsible stunt by a private plane pilot tragically ended Rhoads' life at age 25.

## The Sound

Immaculate technique, including tapping, trills, and hammer-ons with classical and hard rock influences were the cornerstones of the Rhoads style. With Ozzy, he played Les Paul and custom guitars, along with signature Jackson models through Marshall amps. Such is the continuing interest in Rhoads that a Marshall 1959 RR amp, based on his original, was debuted in 2008. Gibson also paid tribute to Rhoads in 2010 when they announced the reissue of Rhoads' 1974 Les Paul Custom.

© Marty Temme

**Guitar:** 1974 Gibson Les Paul Custom, **Karl Sandoval Flying V with Danelectro neck and DiMarzio pickups,** 1982 Jackson Signature Randy Rhoads Concorde model

**Amp:** Marshall 1959 Plexi Super Lead and JMP 100-watt heads with 4x12 cabinets containing Altec speakers

**Effects:** Vox VA47A wah, Roland RE-301 Space Echo Tape Delay, MXR Distortion +, M-108 Graphic EQ, M-117R Flanger and M-134 Stereo Chorus

# TONY RICE

© Erika Goldring / Retna Ltd.

Virginia native **David Anthony "Tony" Rice** (1951– ) is a virtuoso progressive bluegrass picker who helped expand the parameters of music in the seventies to become the jazzy "spacegrass." His father, a semi-professional player, got him started, and Rice was profoundly influenced by Clarence White in the Kentucky Colonels. In 1970, he moved to Kentucky where he joined J.D. Crowe's New South on guitar and vocals. In 1975, he relocated to California to join the David Grisman Quintet for their landmark, self-titled debut. In 1979, he went solo while forming various groups and won a Grammy playing with New South for Best Country Instrumental Performance (1983) for "Fireball." Unfortunately, damage to his vocal cords now prevents him from singing, but his playing is as spectacular as ever.

## The Sound

Bluegrass, country, folk, and jazz intermingle freely and uniquely in the acoustic flatpicking style of Rice. He has studied and learned to read music, allowing himself to be influenced by Miles Davis and John Coltrane, as well as Clarence White. Besides his iconic 1935 Martin D-28, he also plays his signature Santa Cruz guitar (first introduced in 1979) that has evolved into the Tony Rice and Tony Rice Pro models.

**Guitar:** 1935 Martin D-28 (previously owned by Clarence White)

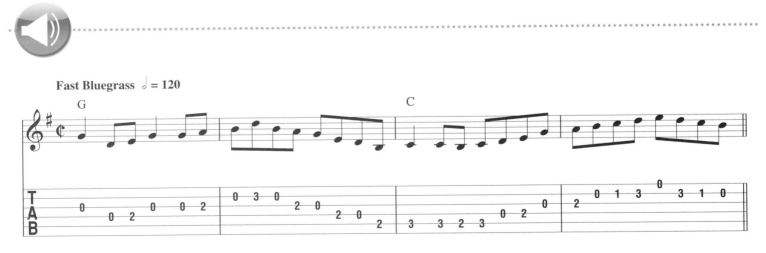

# KEITH RICHARDS

© Photofest

The incomparable, indomitable, and notorious **Keith Richards** (1943– ) arrived with the Rolling Stones during the British Invasion and is still going strong despite five drug-related brushes with the law. First inspired by Scotty Moore, he was substantially influenced by Chuck Berry and the blues of Muddy Waters and Robert Johnson. The original Rolling Stones with the late Brian Jones formed in 1962 and have been declared the "World's Greatest Rock & Roll Band," racking up innumerable awards and accomplishments. Richards has occasionally played outside the Stones, releasing two solo albums with the X-Pensive Winos: the gold *Talk Is Cheap* (1987) and *Main Offender* (1992). The Stones were inducted into the Rock and Roll Hall of Fame in 1989. Richards' autobiography, *Life*, was published in 2010.

## The Sound

Rock rhythm guitarist par excellence, Richards has maintained a consistently gritty, yet defined tone straight into the amp. He is a traditionalist with his gear, as well as his taste in American roots music. Les Pauls and Telecasters have been his main axes, with the Teles serving as his open G guitars. Amps include black-face and tweed Fenders with Vox and the Ampeg SVT (in the seventies) also being heard.

**Guitar:** 1959 Gibson Les Paul Standard, 1957 Gibson Les Paul Custom, **1953 Fender Telecaster**, 1975 Fender Telecaster Custom

**Amp:** 1964 Fender Dual Showman, Mesa Boogie Mark 1 A804, tweed Fender Twin

**Effects:** Gibson Maestro Fuzztone (on "Satisfaction" in 1965)

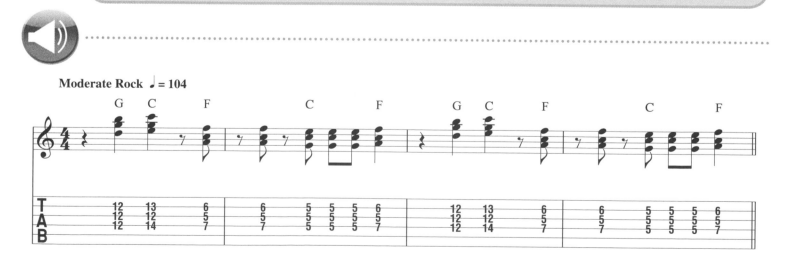

# RICHIE SAMBORA

The fiery guitarist contributing to the success of fellow New Jerseyan Jon Bon Jovi, **Richard Stephen Sambora** (1959– ) began playing at age 12 following the death of Jimi Hendrix. Further influenced by Eric Clapton, Jeff Beck, Johnny Winter, and Spanish classical music, he played with Poison and Message before talking his way into an audition with Bon Jovi in 1983, replacing Dave Sabo in time for their eponymous debut in 1984. Their breakout, pop/hair metal classic *Slippery When Wet* (#1 in 1986) produced "You Give Love a Bad Name," "Livin' on a Prayer," and "Wanted Dead or Alive" featuring Sambora's electric and acoustic skills that are evident down to *The Circle* (#1 in 2009). He has released two solo albums: *Stranger in This Town* (1991) and *Undiscovered Soul* (1998).

## The Sound

Sambora is an avid collector who has utilized a ton of gear to produce a wide variety of electric and acoustic tones. In 1987, Kramer produced a signature Strat-type, and in 1996 and 1997, Fender released the Richie Sambora Black Paisley Strat and Telecaster, respectively. Marshall amps were, of course, de rigueur for eighties metal bands, as were rack mounts and MIDI rigs such as those by Bob Bradshaw that Sambora employed.

© Marty Temme

**Guitar:** Charvel Strat-type, Kramer Richie Sambora Strat-type, Fender Signature Stratocaster, 1959 Gibson Les Paul Standard, **Ovation Adamas** single-, double-neck, and triple-neck models

**Amp:** Marshall 800 100-watt heads, KMD 2x12 combo

**Effects:** Eventide H3000 Harmonizer, Juice Goose PD-2, Roland SDE-1000 digital delay, SPX 9011, TC Electronic 1210 Spatial Expander/Stereo-Chorus Flanger, Rocktron 300A compressor/limiter

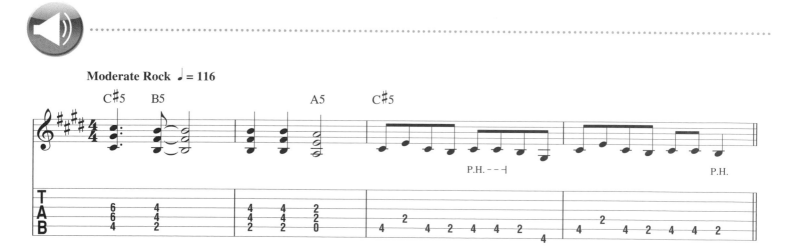

# CARLOS SANTANA

The king of Latin rock, Mexican-born **Carlos Santana** (1947– ) is one of the greatest instrumentalists in any genre. After changing from violin to the guitar at age eight and playing in the bars of Tijuana, Carlos later joined his family in San Francisco in 1963. Seeing B.B. King in 1966 would have a profound effect on Santana, and he would quickly form the Santana Blues Band (soon shortened to simply Santana) and played at Woodstock in 1969 prior to the release of *Santana* (#4) with the hit "Evil Ways" (#9). *Abraxas* (#4) followed in 1970 with "Black Magic Woman" (#4), making Santana a major star. He has gone on to win 10 Grammys and was inducted with his original band into the Rock and Roll Hall of Fame in 1998.

## The Sound

Known as the "cry," the long sustain emanating from the guitars of Santana is one of the most recognizable signature sounds. It took going from an SG Special with P-90 pickups to a Les Paul Standard and a Yamaha SG2000 through a Mesa Boogie amp to produce it. When Santana first played the Randall Smith hot-rodded Fender Princeton prototype around 1970, he exclaimed, "Shit, man. That little thing really boogies!"

© Marty Temme

**Guitar:** Sixties Gibson SG Special, Gibson Les Paul Standard, Gibson L6-S, 1977 Yamaha SG2000, **1995 Paul Reed Smith re-issue**

**Amp:** Black-face Fender Twin Reverb, Mesa Boogie Mark 1, Dumble Overdrive Special

**Effects:** Mu-tron volume/wah-wah pedal

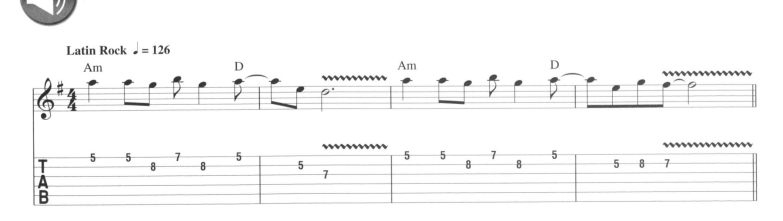

# JOE SATRIANI

© Marty Temme

Long Island native **Joseph "Satch" Satriani** (1956– ) used his technical ability to become a famous teacher and shredding instrumentalist. Inspired by Jimi Hendrix, he began playing guitar and drums at age 14. Satriani became friends with his student, Steve Vai, and moved to Berkeley in 1978 where he taught Kirk Hammett and Charlie Hunter, among others. In the early eighties, he played with Greg Kihn, released an EP, and caught a break when Vai backed David Lee Roth in 1986 and gave Satriani kudos. Concurrently, he released *Not of This Earth* to be followed by the even more spectacular gold *Surfing with the Alien* (#29 in 1987) featuring "Satch Boogie" (#22). In 2008, he formed Chickenfoot with Sammy Hagar and Michael Anthony (Van Halen) and Chad Smith (Red Hot Chili Peppers).

## The Sound

Satriani utilizes legato hammer-ons and pull-offs, tapping, and whammy bar manipulation in conjunction with his theory of improvising with modes called "pitch axis," often playing exceedingly fast with soaring sustain. He has long been an endorsee of Ibanez guitars, and they have released many different electrics with P-90, DiMarzio, and Seymour Duncan pickups, as well as several acoustic models. Likewise, he also has an endorsement deal with Peavey amps and Vox effects.

**Guitar:** Ibanez 540 Radius, **Ibanez JS2CH "Chrome Boy"**, 1958 Fender Esquire
**Amp:** Peavey Classic, Marshall 6100 LM, Peavey Signature JSX, Mini Colossal
**Effects:** Vox Signature "Saturator" distortion, "Time Machine" delay, "Big Bad Wah," and "Ice 9" overdrive pedals

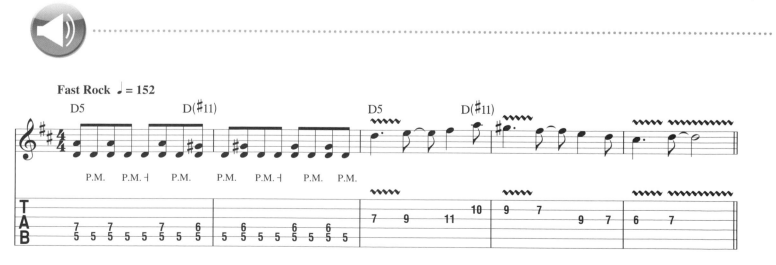

# MICHAEL SCHENKER

© Chrysalis / Photofest

German rock god **Michael Schenker** (1955– ) is an unsung pioneering hero of hard rock. He was influenced by his older brother Rudolph (the Scorpions) and was sitting in with them by age 15 and appearing on *Lonesome Crow* (1972). When he joined UFO for *Phenomenon* (1974), he possessed exceptional chops, expressiveness, and melodic ideas. After three albums, including *Lights Out* (#23 in 1977), he left in 1979 to rejoin the Scorpions. Following *Lovedrive* (1979), he split, unsuccessfully auditioning with Aerosmith for Joe Perry's job. He went on to release many solo albums with the Michael Schenker Group (MSG) and McAuley-Schenker Group. In 1993, he rejoined UFO for *Walk on Water* (1995) and once again in 2002 for *Sharks*.

## The Sound

Blues feel and phrasing has always been a significant element in Schenker's melodic playing. As opposed to other heavy rockers, he employs a relatively unencumbered Marshall-powered distortion that emphasizes his vibrato, though he uses a wah pedal as a tone modifier. His iconic guitar is a custom black/white painted seventies Gibson Flying V. Since 2004, Dean Guitars has brought out an extensive series of signature electric and acoustic instruments.

**Guitar: 1975 Gibson Flying V**, 1979 Gibson Flying V, Dean Signature model

**Amp:** Marshall JCM 800 2205 50-watt head with Marshall 912M cabinet

**Effects:** Cry Baby wah, Boss DD-3 Digital Delay and CE-5 Chorus Ensemble, Marshall Delay/Chorus

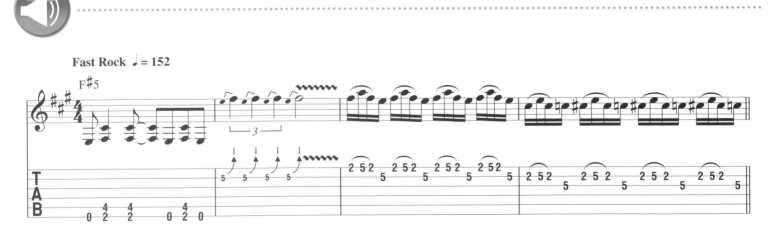

# TOM SCHOLZ

**Donald Thomas "Tom" Scholz** (1947– ) is, literally, the brains behind Boston. As a child, he studied classical piano, graduated with a master's degree in mechanical engineering from MIT in 1970, and went to work for Polaroid. He produced demos in his home studio; these later became tracks for the phenomenal debut Boston album (#3 in 1976) featuring "More Than a Feeling" (#5) and "Peace of Mind" (#38). It took two years for the follow-up, *Don't Look Back*, and after *Third Stage* (#3 in 1986), Scholz engaged in long litigation with CBS records. *Corporate America* (#42 in 2002) expressed his outrage at the record industry. In 1981, he formed Scholz Research & Design (sold to Dunlop in 1995), inventing the Rockman headphone amp and the Power Soak.

## The Sound

Scholz, for all his technical expertise, has been a confirmed analog man with vintage gear including two 1968 Les Paul guitars that he favors for their large necks. Before he invented the Rockman line of gear, he used Marshall amps and a homemade power attenuator to access the sound and sustain at manageable volume levels. In addition, he played through a wah pedal set in one position to enhance the midrange.

> **Guitar:** 1968 Gibson Les Paul Goldtop with P-90 pickups and **1968 Gibson Les Paul Goldtop with DiMarzio Super Distortion humbuckers**
>
> **Amp:** Seventies Marshall 100-watt stack
>
> **Effects:** Power attenuator, Vox wah

© Photofest

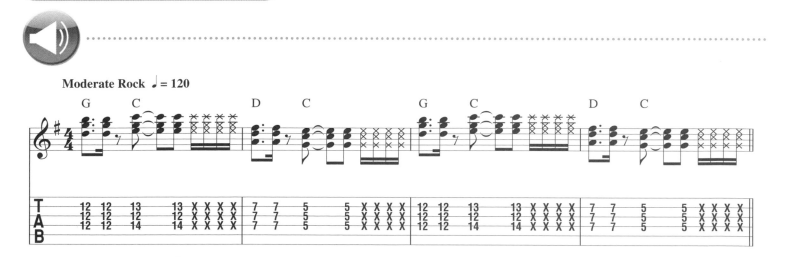

# SLASH

**Saul "Slash" Hudson** (1965– ) was born in England but raised in Hollywood. Inspired by the Stones and Aerosmith, he began playing in junior high where he met drummer Steven Adler. They would eventually join up with singer Axl Rose, guitarist Izzy Stradlin, and bassist Duff McKagan for Guns N' Roses in 1985. Their major label debut, *Appetite for Destruction* (#1 in 1987), containing "Sweet Child O' Mine" (#1), "Welcome to the Jungle" (#7), and "Paradise City" (#5), revitalized hard rock. Slash would be featured until 1996 when his substance abuse, conflicts with Rose, and a desire to rock harder compelled him to quit. He formed Slash's Snakepit and Velvet Revolver, the latter to some acclaim, and released his self-titled first solo album in 2010.

## The Sound

Slash is a contemporary Les Paul guitar hero with chops to back it up. He has likewise taken advantage of the thick, deep tone and superior sustain of the heavy instrument to express his melodic and bluesy phrasing in the manner of his predecessors. Combined with a Marshall stack, he produces one of the great, gritty, hard rock sounds, augmented by the wah pedal and tasteful delay.

© Marty Iemme

**Guitar:** Chris Derrig reproduction 1959 Gibson Les Paul Standard with Alnico II Pro pickups, 1987 Gibson Les Paul Standard ("Patti") with Duncan Alnico II Pro pickups, **2010 Gibson USA Slash Les Paul Standard**

**Amp:** Tim Caswell (from SIR Studios in L.A.) modified 1965–73 Marshall Super Tremolo, 1959T 100-watt head, Marshall JCM 800

**Effects:** Boss DD-3 digital delay, MXR graphic equalizer, Dunlop Cry Baby wah

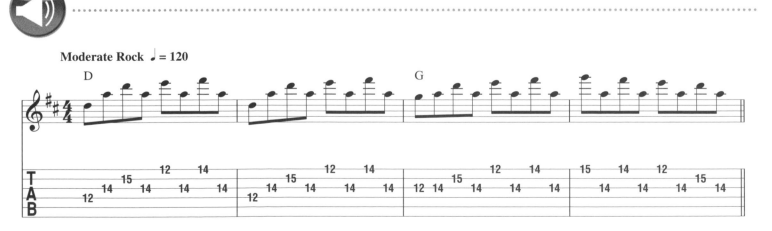

# ANDY SUMMERS

© Pictorial Press Ltd / Alamy

The unique and inventive Brit **Andrew James Somers** (1942– ) started playing at age 14. By 17, inspired by Django Reinhardt and Wes Montgomery, he was gigging on the local jazz scene and in 1968–69 played briefly with Soft Machine and the Animals. From 1969–73, he lived in Southern California and studied classical guitar at UCLA. Back in England, he changed his name, backed up various artists, and met Sting and Stewart Copeland in Strontium 90 in 1977. They formed the Police, and Summers won a Best Rock Instrumental Grammy for "Behind My Camel" (1980), even though Sting refused to play on it. In 1984, the Police broke up, and Summers commenced a solo career, playing on soundtracks and collaborating with Robert Fripp, among others. The Police reunited in 2007–08.

## The Sound

With chops far in advance of his fellow "new wavers" in the eighties, Summers has a legacy of memorable melodies, sophisticated chord voicings, and an iconic tone. A Tele-master who basically sidestepped the typical country/rockabilly twang, he nonetheless forged a swirling, signature sound with judicious effects such as flanging, phasing, and echo. He also played several Gibson guitars through hot-rodded Marshall amps. Fender introduced the Andy Summers Tribute Telecaster in 2008.

**Guitar:** 1961 Fender Telecaster Custom with PAF humbucker, 1961 Fender Stratocaster, 1958 and 1964 Gibson ES-175, Roland G-303 guitar synthesizer, Gibson Chet Atkins electric classical

**Amp:** Modified Marshall 100-watt half-stack, Roland Jazz Chorus

**Effects:** Maestro Echoplex, Pete Cornish pedal board (MXR Dyna Comp, Phase 90, Analog Delay, Electro-Harmonix Electric Mistress Flanger/Filter Matrix and Big Muff Pi, Mu-tron III Envelope Follower)

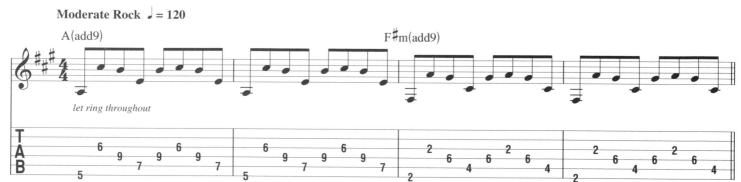

# PETE TOWNSHEND

© Pictorial Press Ltd / Alamy

**Peter Dennis Blandford Townshend** (1945– ) is the incomparable creative force behind the British rock powerhouse the Who. His parents were both musical, and he received his first guitar at age 12, while also playing banjo. Link Wray and Hank Marvin were early influences, and Townshend attended art school in 1962 while his friend, John Entwistle, played with Roger Daltrey in the Detours. Towns-hend joined them in 1963, and with the arrival of Keith Moon in 1964, they became the Who. "I Can't Explain" (#8 in 1965—with Jimmy Page) was their first single, and their explosive stage act developed. They were inducted into the Rock and Roll Hall of Fame in 1990, and Townshend and Daltrey have continued on together and individually following the death of Moon (1978) and Entwistle (2002).

## The Sound

Following his experiments with feedback, as first heard on "Anyway, Anyhow, Anywhere" (1965), Townshend wanted more volume and had Jim Marshall build a 100-watt head with an 8x12 speaker cabinet that was quickly cut into two 4x12 cabinets—this became the "classic" Marshall rig. He would also play Sound City and Hiwatt amps, as well as Fenders. Rickenbackers, Strats, and Gibson SGs and Les Pauls would be his main squeezes.

**Guitar:** 1965 Rickenbacker Rose, Morris Co. 1997 model, **1968 Gibson SG Special**, 1971 Gibson Les Paul Deluxe, 1959 Gretsch 6120, Fender Electric XII 12-string, 1968 Gibson J-200

**Amp:** 1964 Fender Bassman, 1965 Marshall 1959 Super Lead 100-watt, Sound City L100, Hiwatt CP103 100-watt, 1959 Fender Bandmaster 3x10

**Effects:** Sola Sound Tone Bender fuzz, Edwards Light Show volume pedal, Marshall Supa Fuzz, Gibson Maestro Fuzz-Tone, Dallas Arbiter Fuzz Face, Univox Super Fuzz

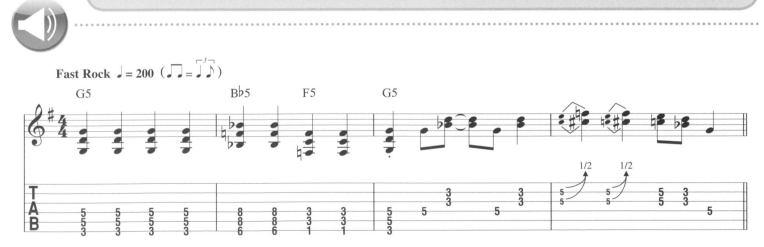

# MERLE TRAVIS

Kentuckian **Merle Robert Travis** (1917–1983) was so influential on country guitar that his contribution became known as "Travis picking." He first played banjo and then guitar at age 12, while being tutored by Ike Everly, and made his first recordings for King Records in Cincinnati before World War II. After serving in the Marines, he moved to L.A. where a contract with Capitol Records (1946) would lead to the modern C&W hits "Sixteen Tons," "Nine Pound Hammer," and "Smoke, Smoke, Smoke (That Cigarette)." He appeared in *From Here to Eternity* (1953) with Frank Sinatra, playing "Re-enlistment Blues." Travis played on *Will the Circle Be Unbroken* (1971) with the Nitty Gritty Dirt Band and won a Grammy for the *Atkins-Travis Traveling Show* (1974). He died of a heart attack at age 65.

## The Sound

"Travis picking" consists of his simultaneous alternating bass-string patterns and treble-string melodies on acoustic or electric guitar. Regarding the latter, Travis had California inventor Paul Bigsby build a custom solidbody guitar for him that has a headstock shaped remarkably like a Strat. He also played a Martin D-28 and a Gibson Super 400 through a variety of amps. In 2008, Martin released a signature D-28 with the Bigsby headstock.

© Photofest

**Guitar:** 1941 Martin D-28, 1946 Bigsby solidbody electric, **1952 Gibson Super 400 with P-90 pickups**
**Amp:** Fifties Standel 25L15

# ROBIN TROWER

British blues rock virtuoso **Robin Leonard Trower** (1945– ) combined electric blues with the chord melody of Jimi Hendrix. He began playing around 1956, inspired by Scotty Moore, Steve Cropper, and Hubert Sumlin. He played in the R&B-style Paramounts in 1960–66 and joined Procol Harum in 1967–71. Opening for Hendrix in 1970 would have a profound effect on Trower after he went solo. His second release, *Bridge of Sighs* (#7 in 1974), was a landmark of neo-psychedelic blues rock and his masterpiece. In 1981–82, he teamed up with Jack Bruce and with Procol Harum in 1991 for *Prodigal Stranger*. After several detours, Trower returned to his roots with *Living out of Time* (2004), *Another Day's Blues* (2005), *What Lies Beneath* (2009), and *The Playful Heart* (2010).

## The Sound

Though unfairly criticized in the press for merely being a Hendrix imitator, Trower forged a signature sound and personal style on the Strat. Part of it is the result of tuning down one or two whole steps. 100-watt Marshall stacks were the concert amp of choice, combined with a modest array of effects, including the crucial Univibe and a wah pedal. Fender introduced a signature model Strat in 2004.

© Chrysalis / Photofest

**Guitar:** 1956 Fender Stratocaster, 1966 Fender Stratocaster, **early-seventies Fender Stratocaster**, 2004 Fender Signature Stratocaster

**Amp:** Marshall JMP 100 Mark II stack

**Effects:** Univox Univibe chorus/vibrato, Tychobrahe wah, Dan Armstrong Red Ranger treble booster, Mu-tron II phase shifter, Electro-Harmonix Electric Mistress

# STEVE VAI

© Marty Temme

Long Island rock wizard **Steven Siro Vai** (1960– ) began playing at age 13, inspired by Jeff Beck, Jimmy Page, and Allan Holdsworth. He studied with Joe Satriani, and later attended the Berklee School of Music in Boston in 1968. In a famous story, Vai sent an unsolicited Zappa transcription to Frank, which led to his role as "stunt" guitarist through 1984. He began his solo career with *Flex-Able* (1984), played in Alcatrazz (1985), joined David Lee Roth (1985), played the devil in *Crossroads* (1986), and starred in Whitesnake (1989), among other projects. He won Grammys for "Sofa" (1993), *No Substitutions: Live in Osaka* (2001), and "Peaches en Regalia" (2008). Vai began the G3 series of tours with Satriani (1996) and founded the Favored Nations label (1999).

## The Sound

*Passion and Warfare* (1990) encapsulates the heavy delay/distortion/sustain sound that made Vai a guitar hero. He played Strats with Zappa, followed by Jackson guitars. Beginning in 1988, Ibanez released a signature series of Strat-type JEM 777 guitars, including a 7-string that is credited with starting a craze among metal guitarists. Vai has utilized a wide range of gear including Marshall and Carvin amps and countless effects, with delay high on the list.

**Guitar:** Tom Anderson custom, **1987 Ibanez JEM 777**, Ibanez JEM-7V 7-string

**Amp:** ADA MP1 preamp, Jose Arredondo-modified Marshall JMP1 head into effects rack and Mesa Boogie Strategy 400 power amp, Yamaha PC2002M power amp

**Effects:** Boss FV-100 volume pedal, Dunlop Cry Baby wah, Furman PL-8 power conditioner, Roland SDE-3000 digital delay, Yamaha D1500 Digital Delay and SPX90 Multieffects, Ibanez SDR1000 Digital Reverb, Eventide H969 Harmonizer and H3000S, Lexicon PCM70 Digital Reverb, Bradshaw switching system

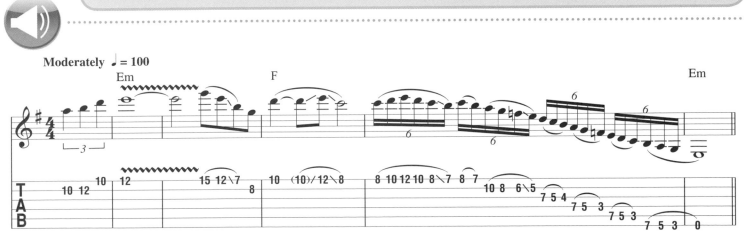

# EDDIE VAN HALEN

© Marty Temme

Dutchman **Eduard Lodewijk Van Halen** (1955– ) moved to Southern California and became one of the most influential rock guitarists of all time. He originally played drums and his brother, Alex, played guitar before they switched and formed Mammoth with bassist Michael Anthony and singer David Lee Roth around 1972; they changed the band name to Van Halen in 1974. Thanks to Gene Simmons, they signed with Warner Bros. (1977), and their debut spawned hordes of Eddie imitators. Platinum sales, five #1 albums, 12 #1 singles, and Grammys for *For Unlawful Carnal Knowledge* (1991) followed. Sammy Hagar would replace Roth, and Eddie would battle alcohol abuse and health problems. Eventually, his son, Wolfgang, would play bass. The band with Roth and Hagar was inducted into the Rock and Roll Hall of Fame in 2007.

## The Sound

Eddie has described his ideal tone as the "brown sound," an apt term for his harmonically-rich humbucker/tube tone. He built a solidbody guitar in the mid seventies, dubbed "Frankenstrat," with a single PAF hardwired to the volume knob for an exceptionally unfiltered sound. Marshall, and later a signature Peavey amp with few effects, complete the sound. In 2004, Charvel released the EVH Artist Series and Fender introduced the Relic "Frankenstrat" in 2007.

**Guitar:** 1976 "Frankenstrat" (seventies Charvel body and neck, one Gibson PAF humbucker, Fender tremolo bridge, single volume knob), **1979 Charvel hybrid**, Ibanez Destroyer, 1983 Kramer 5150, 1991 Ernie Ball/Music Man signature model, 1996 Peavey EVH Wolfgang, 2004 Charvel EVH Art Series

**Amp:** 1967 Marshall, 1959 Super Lead 100-watt head with single 12" Celestion cabinet and Variac, Peavey 5150

**Effects:** MXR Phase 90, Flanger, and 6-Band EQ; Echoplex-Maestro EP-3 tape delay, Boss GE-10 Graphic EQ

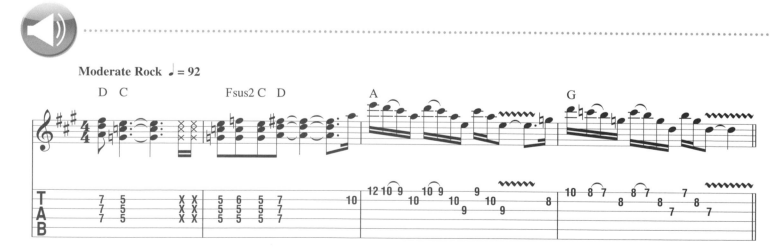

Moderate Rock ♩ = 92

# STEVIE RAY VAUGHAN

The greatest contemporary electric blues guitarist, Texan **Stevie Ray Vaughan** (1954–1990), was first influenced by his older brother Jimmie. He dropped out of high school at age 17 to play in the Cobras and was leading Double Trouble with bassist Tommy Shannon and drummer Chris Layton by 1978. Playing the Montreux Festival in 1982 led to a gig for Vaughan and free recording time for the band with David Bowie and Jackson Browne, respectively. John Hammond, Sr. secured a contract and *Texas Flood* (1983) helped create a new blues revival. Four more albums followed as Vaughan became a cherished guitar hero, while dealing with substance abuse. He died tragically in a helicopter crash at age 36, after getting straight. Eight posthumous albums would reach #1 on the blues charts.

## The Sound

Combining his thorough knowledge of the blues with a love for Jimi Hendrix, Vaughan created a guitar-into-amp, fat Strat tone augmented with select effects. A good deal of his tone came from his heavy gauge strings, oversized frets, and extreme volume. Marshall, Fender, and Soldano amps were his choice, though he continued to experiment through to *In Step* with assistance from "amp doctor" Cesar Diaz. In 1992, Fender introduced a signature Strat.

© Photofest

**Guitar:** 1963 Fender Stratocaster ("Number One") with '62 neck and '59 pickups, 1962 Fender Stratocaster ("Red"), 1962–63 Fender Stratocaster ("Lenny"), 1958 Gibson ES-335

**Amp:** Marshall 4140 JMP Club and Country 100-watt combo with two 12" speakers, 1963 Fender Vibroverb

**Effects:** Ibanez TS-808 Tube Screamer, Cry Baby wah, Dallas Arbiter Fuzz Face, Tychobrahe Octavia

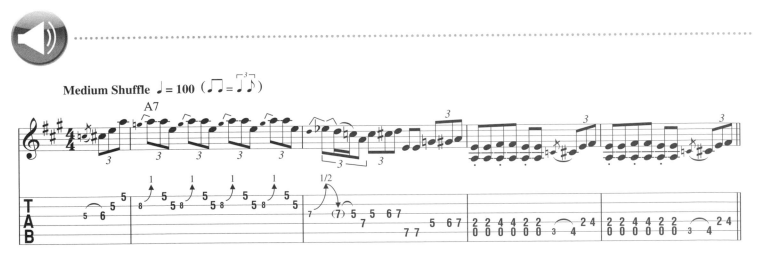

# T-BONE WALKER

The "Father of Electric Blues," Texan **Aaron Thie-beault Walker** (1910–1975) remains one of the greatest. His stepfather played the bass fiddle, and young Walker met bluesmen like Blind Lemon Jefferson. As "Oak Cliff T-Bone," he waxed "Wichita Falls Blues" b/w "Trinity River Blues" (1929). Both he and his friend, Charlie Christian, studied with Chuck Richardson in Oklahoma City (1933). He moved to Los Angeles in 1935 where he used his singing, dancing, and instrumental talents to acclaim. The paradigm changed when he recorded "I Got a Break, Baby" b/w "Mean Old World" (1942). "Call It Stormy Monday" (1947) is the best-known of his many post-war classics. Walker died from a stroke at age 64, and was posthumously inducted into the Rock and Roll Hall of Fame in 1987.

## The Sound

Walker epitomizes the vibrant, cutting sound of a hollowbody Gibson directly into the amp with no reverb. The earliest photos show him with the ES-250. The fancy ES-5 with three P-90 pickups, however, has become his iconic axe and was reportedly his favorite. An early fifties Fender Pro amp with a 15" speaker proved a magical combination with the ES-5.

© Michael Ochs Archive / Getty Images

**Guitar:** 1939 Gibson ES-250, late-forties Gibson ES-300, **1952 Gibson ES-5**
**Amp:** Gibson EH-185, 1952 Fender Pro

# JOHNNY WINTER

© Marty Temme

Texas blues legend **John Dawson Winter III** (1944–2014) played ukulele in a duo with his brother, Edgar, in the early fifties. By the mid fifties, he was playing guitar and learning the solos of T-Bone Walker, Muddy Waters, Chuck Berry, and Carl Perkins, along with Robert Johnson slide licks. In 1968, a feature story in *Rolling Stone* led to a blockbuster contract with Columbia Records. *Johnny Winter* and *Second Winter* (1969) began an ongoing blues career with forays into rock. He played at Woodstock, but his management kept the footage out of the hit movie; a release of his set (2010) reached #1. *Live: Johnny Winter And* (1971) remains his best-selling release while *Still Alive and Well* (1973) aptly summed up his recovery from drug abuse.

## The Sound

Winter has always gravitated toward a bright, trebly Texas blues sound with bite. To reach that end, he went through a variety of guitars, including an Epiphone Wilshire, Les Paul Custom, Fender Electric XII 12-string converted to a 6-string, and most prominently, his iconic reverse Firebird, which was released as a signature model in 2008. Amps have included a Fender Super Reverb, Marshall, Ampeg, and later Music Man amps with an MXR Phase 90.

**Guitar:** Early sixties Gibson Les Paul/SG, late-sixties Fender Electric XII 12-string solidbody with six strings, **1963 Gibson Firebird V**

**Amp:** Tweed Fender Bassman, sixties black-face Fender Super Reverb

**Effects:** Cry Baby wah, Univox Univibe

# ZAKK WYLDE

© Robert Knight

**Jeffrey Phillip "Zakk Wylde" Weidlant** (1967– ) has played with Ozzy Osbourne on and off since 1987 and was voted "Most Valuable Player" for three consecutive years in *Guitar World*. The bluesy metal guitarist began at age eight, became serious in his teens, studied classical music, and gigged at the Jersey shore. He formed Stonehenge in 1984 and debuted with Ozzy on *No Rest for the Wicked* (1988), continuing on until he split to start Pride & Glory in 1994 for one self-titled album. After an audition with Guns N' Roses, Wylde went solo with extra Pride & Glory material for *Book of Shadows* (1996), followed by *Sonic Brew* (1999) with the Black Label Society. The latter's *Order of the Black* hit #4 in 2010.

## The Sound

Classic Marshall roar, not overly compressed, with a Southern accent, typifies classic Wylde. When he joined Ozzy, he wanted to distinguish himself visually, as well as aurally, from Randy Rhoads, so he had Gibson put iconic bull's-eye graphics (and others) on his Les Paul Custom guitars. The EMG pickups facilitate the pinched harmonics that Wylde is known for, and the Rotovibe, Phase 90, and Chorus Ensemble add color to his big humbucker/Marshall sound.

---

**Guitar:** Signature Gibson Les Paul Custom Bull's-eye with EMG 81 and 85 pickups, Signature Gibson Les Paul Custom Buzzsaw, Signature Gibson Flying V, Signature Dean Razorback

**Amp:** Marshall JCM 800 with 1960 TV cabinets

**Effects:** Dunlop Jimi Hendrix wah, Signature Dunlop ZW-45 wah pedal and JD-4S Rotovibe Expression pedal, Signature MXR Overdrive, EVH Phase 90 and Chorus, Boss Super Overdrive SD-1 and CE-5 Chorus Ensemble

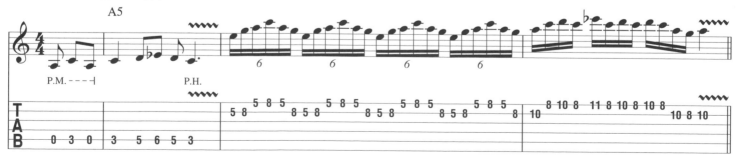

# ANGUS YOUNG

Scottish-born guitarist **Angus McKinnon Young** (1955– ) has led the hard-rocking Australian band AC/DC with his brother Malcolm since 1973; their older brother, George, was in the Easybeats (of "Friday on My Mind" fame). With lead singer Bon Scott, they developed a reputation for rowdiness, to go with their uncompromising power chord attack. Following *Highway to Hell* (1979), Scott died of alcohol poisoning in 1980. His replacement, Brian Johnson, contributed to their greatest success, *Back in Black* (1980) and *For Those About to Rock, We Salute You* (1981); the latter hit #1 in the U.S. Lean years were highlighted by *Ballbreaker* (1995), their induction into the Rock and Roll Hall of Fame in 2003, and a comeback with *Black Ice* (2008) that won a Grammy for "War Machine" (2009).

## The Sound

What Slash is to the Les Paul/Marshall combination, Young is to the SG/Marshall combination. As influenced by the blues and Chuck Berry, Young plays straight into the amp with virtually no effects except for a wireless system that allows him to perform his various stage antics. In 2009, Gibson brought out a signature model with a signature humbucker that Young designed for the bridge and a '57 Classic in the neck position.

> **Guitar:** 1968 Gibson SG Standard with replaced "Lyre" vibrato tailpiece
>
> **Amp:** Marshall JCM 800, JMP and JTM 45 heads, Marshall Super Lead, 1959 Plexi 100-watt stack

© Marty Temme

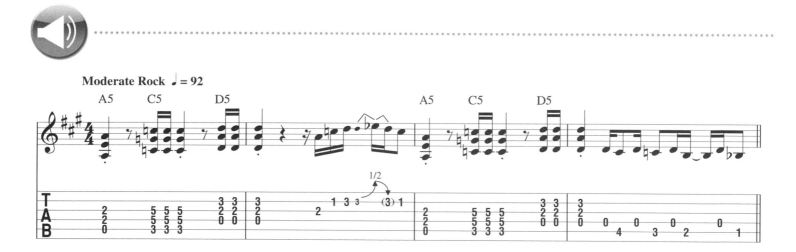

# NEIL YOUNG

Canadian folk and rock guitar legend **Neil Percival "Shakey" Young** (1945– ) went from the Toronto folk scene to L.A. in 1967 to form the Buffalo Springfield with Stephen Stills. Though critically acclaimed, internal tension broke them up after three albums. Following *After the Gold Rush* (1968) and *Everybody Knows This Is Nowhere* (1969), he joined Crosby, Stills & Nash, and they won a Grammy for Best New Artist. He would reunite with CSNY intermittently while creating an ongoing, spectacular career highlighted by *Harvest* (#1 in 1972). Young was inducted into the Rock and Roll Hall of Fame solo (1995) and with the Springfield (1997). Recovery from a brain aneurysm (2005) impelled him to produce even more, including the avant-garde *Le Noise* (2010).

## The Sound

Young is an accomplished "clawhammer" acoustic guitarist and well known as the "Godfather of Grunge" for his heavy, distortion-laden, iconic Les Paul. He played hollow Gretsch guitars in the Buffalo Springfield before acquiring "Old Black," a Les Paul that he modified with a Bigsby vibrato, a P-90 pickup in the neck, and a Firebird pickup in the bridge. His vintage Martin D-28 was previously owned by Hank Williams.

© Marty Temme

**Guitar:** 1953 Gibson Les Paul Goldtop painted black ("Old Black"), 1966 Gretsch 6120, 1961 Gretsch White Falcon, early forties Martin D-28 ("Hank"), 1968 Martin D-45

**Amp:** 1959 Tweed Fender Deluxe, fifties Magnatone 280 Stereo

**Effects:** Remote footswitch controlled "Whizzer" to turn volume and tone knobs on the Fender Deluxe, Fender outboard tube reverb unit, Maestro EP-4 Echoplex, MXR M-118 Analog delay

# FRANK ZAPPA

Born in Maryland and raised in California, **Frank Vincent Zappa** (1940–1993) was a wildly creative composer and underrated rock guitarist, as heard on *Shut Up 'N Play Yer Guitar* (1981). He played drums before switching to guitar, and his broad musical interests ranged from R&B, doo-wop, and jazz to the avant-garde composer Edgar Varese. *Freak Out!* (1966), with the Mothers of Invention, was a landmark of sixties eclecticism. Zappa would go on to push the boundaries of music and taste while remaining a staunch defender of freedom of speech, winning Grammys for *Jazz from Hell* (1987) and *Civilization Phaze III* (1995). Zappa died prematurely at age 52 from prostate cancer and was posthumously inducted into the Rock and Roll Hall of Fame in 1995.

## The Sound

Zappa owned and played a burned Jimi Hendrix 1965 Strat from the 1968 Miami Pop Festival, which was given to him by a tech, and his son, Dweezil, rebuilt it in the eighties. After the Gibson ES-5 Switchmaster that he played early in the Mothers, Zappa's guitars, including Gibson SGs, Les Pauls, and Fender Strats, became heavily modified with various pickups and preamps. He experimented with countless amps and effects in search of the rawest, weirdest tones.

© Marty Temme

**Guitar:** Fifties ES-5 Switchmaster, 1952–53 customized Gibson Les Paul Goldtop, Custom seventies SG-type ("Baby Snakes"), **late-sixties Gibson SG**, late-seventies modified Gibson Les Paul Custom with Duncan pickups, Performance Guitars custom Strat-type with DiMarzio pickups

**Amp:** Seventies Pignose, seventies Acoustic 270 bass head, 1978 Marshall Super Lead 100-watt stack, Marshall JCM 800 with two 1x12 EV cabinets

**Effects:** Cry Baby wah, Electro Wagnerian Emancipator, Mu-tron Biphase, Oberheim VCF voltage control filter, Eventide 949 Harmonizer, DBX 162 stereo compressor, MicMix Dynaflanger, Aphex Expressor Compressor

# GUITAR NOTATION LEGEND

Guitar music can be notated three different ways: on a *musical staff*, in *tablature*, and in *rhythm slashes*.

**RHYTHM SLASHES** are written above the staff. Strum chords in the rhythm indicated. Use the chord diagrams found at the top of the first page of the transcription for the appropriate chord voicings. Round noteheads indicate single notes.

**THE MUSICAL STAFF** shows pitches and rhythms and is divided by bar lines into measures. Pitches are named after the first seven letters of the alphabet.

**TABLATURE** graphically represents the guitar fingerboard. Each horizontal line represents a string, and each number represents a fret.

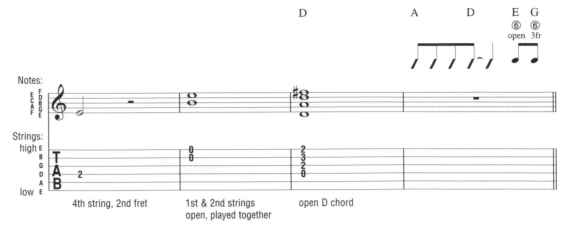

4th string, 2nd fret     1st & 2nd strings open, played together     open D chord

## Definitions for Special Guitar Notation

**HALF-STEP BEND:** Strike the note and bend up 1/2 step.

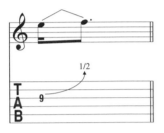

**WHOLE-STEP BEND:** Strike the note and bend up one step.

**GRACE NOTE BEND:** Strike the note and immediately bend up as indicated.

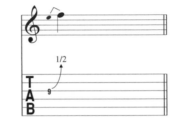

**SLIGHT (MICROTONE) BEND:** Strike the note and bend up 1/4 step.

**BEND AND RELEASE:** Strike the note and bend up as indicated, then release back to the original note. Only the first note is struck.

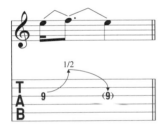

**PRE-BEND:** Bend the note as indicated, then strike it.

**PRE-BEND AND RELEASE:** Bend the note as indicated. Strike it and release the bend back to the original note.

**UNISON BEND:** Strike the two notes simultaneously and bend the lower note up to the pitch of the higher.

**VIBRATO:** The string is vibrated by rapidly bending and releasing the note with the fretting hand.

**WIDE VIBRATO:** The pitch is varied to a greater degree by vibrating with the fretting hand.

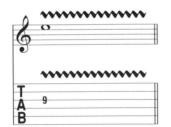

**HAMMER-ON:** Strike the first (lower) note with one finger, then sound the higher note (on the same string) with another finger by fretting it without picking.

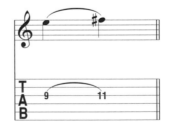

**PULL-OFF:** Place both fingers on the notes to be sounded. Strike the first note and without picking, pull the finger off to sound the second (lower) note.

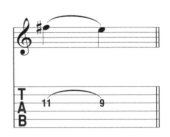

**LEGATO SLIDE:** Strike the first note and then slide the same fret-hand finger up or down to the second note. The second note is not struck.

**SHIFT SLIDE:** Same as legato slide, except the second note is struck.

**TRILL:** Very rapidly alternate between the notes indicated by continuously hammering on and pulling off.

**TAPPING:** Hammer ("tap") the fret indicated with the pick-hand index or middle finger and pull off to the note fretted by the fret hand.

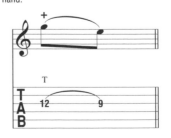

**NATURAL HARMONIC:** Strike the note while the fret-hand lightly touches the string directly over the fret indicated.

**PINCH HARMONIC:** The note is fretted normally and a harmonic is produced by adding the edge of the thumb or the tip of the index finger of the pick hand to the normal pick attack.

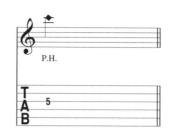

**HARP HARMONIC:** The note is fretted normally and a harmonic is produced by gently resting the pick hand's index finger directly above the indicated fret (in parentheses) while the pick hand's thumb or pick assists by plucking the appropriate string.

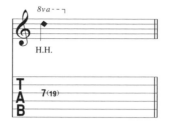

**PICK SCRAPE:** The edge of the pick is rubbed down (or up) the string, producing a scratchy sound.

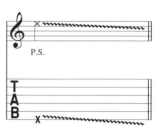

**MUFFLED STRINGS:** A percussive sound is produced by laying the fret hand across the string(s) without depressing, and striking them with the pick hand.

**PALM MUTING:** The note is partially muted by the pick hand lightly touching the string(s) just before the bridge.

**RAKE:** Drag the pick across the strings indicated with a single motion.

**TREMOLO PICKING:** The note is picked as rapidly and continuously as possible.

**ARPEGGIATE:** Play the notes of the chord indicated by quickly rolling them from bottom to top.

**VIBRATO BAR DIVE AND RETURN:** The pitch of the note or chord is dropped a specified number of steps (in rhythm), then returned to the original pitch.

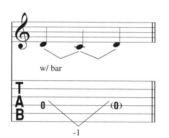

**VIBRATO BAR SCOOP:** Depress the bar just before striking the note, then quickly release the bar.

**VIBRATO BAR DIP:** Strike the note and then immediately drop a specified number of steps, then release back to the original pitch.

# Additional Musical Definitions

| | | |
|---|---|---|
| > (accent) | • Accentuate note (play it louder). | |
| ^ (accent) | • Accentuate note with great intensity. | |
| ⋅ (staccato) | • Play the note short. | |
| ⊓ | • Downstroke | |
| V | • Upstroke | |

**D.S. al Coda** — • Go back to the sign (%), then play until the measure marked "*To Coda*," then skip to the section labelled "**Coda**."

**D.C. al Fine** — • Go back to the beginning of the song and play until the measure marked "*Fine*" (end).

**Rhy. Fig.** — • Label used to recall a recurring accompaniment pattern (usually chordal).

**Riff** — • Label used to recall composed, melodic lines (usually single notes) which recur.

**Fill** — • Label used to identify a brief melodic figure which is to be inserted into the arrangement.

**Rhy. Fill** — • A chordal version of a Fill.

**tacet** — • Instrument is silent (drops out).

• Repeat measures between signs.

• When a repeated section has different endings, play the first ending only the first time and the second ending only the second time.

**NOTE:** Tablature numbers in parentheses mean:
1. The note is being sustained over a system (note in standard notation is tied), or
2. The note is sustained, but a new articulation (such as a hammer-on, pull-off, slide or vibrato) begins, or
3. The note is a barely audible "ghost" note (note in standard notation is also in parentheses).

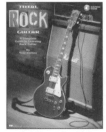

# HAL•LEONARD® GUITAR PLAY-ALONG

AUDIO ACCESS INCLUDED

This series will help you play your favorite songs quickly and easily. Just follow the tab and listen to the audio to the hear how the guitar should sound, and then play along using the separate backing tracks. Audio files also include software to slow down the tempo without changing pitch. The melody and lyrics are included in the book so that you can sing or simply follow along.

**INCLUDES TAB**

| | |
|---|---|
| VOL. 1 – ROCK | 00699570 / $16.99 |
| VOL. 2 – ACOUSTIC | 00699569 / $16.99 |
| VOL. 3 – HARD ROCK | 00699573 / $17.99 |
| VOL. 4 – POP/ROCK | 00699571 / $16.99 |
| VOL. 6 – '90S ROCK | 00699572 / $16.99 |
| VOL. 7 – BLUES | 00699575 / $17.99 |
| VOL. 8 – ROCK | 00699585 / $16.99 |
| VOL. 9 – EASY ACOUSTIC SONGS | 00151708 / $16.99 |
| VOL. 10 – ACOUSTIC | 00699586 / $16.95 |
| VOL. 11 – EARLY ROCK | 00699579 / $14.95 |
| VOL. 12 – POP/ROCK | 00699587 / $14.95 |
| VOL. 13 – FOLK ROCK | 00699581 / $16.99 |
| VOL. 14 – BLUES ROCK | 00699582 / $16.99 |
| VOL. 15 – R&B | 00699583 / $16.99 |
| VOL. 16 – JAZZ | 00699584 / $15.95 |
| VOL. 17 – COUNTRY | 00699588 / $16.99 |
| VOL. 18 – ACOUSTIC ROCK | 00699577 / $15.95 |
| VOL. 19 – SOUL | 00699578 / $15.99 |
| VOL. 20 – ROCKABILLY | 00699580 / $16.99 |
| VOL. 21 – SANTANA | 00174525 / $17.99 |
| VOL. 22 – CHRISTMAS | 00699600 / $15.99 |
| VOL. 23 – SURF | 00699635 / $15.99 |
| VOL. 24 – ERIC CLAPTON | 00699649 / $17.99 |
| VOL. 25 – THE BEATLES | 00198265 / $17.99 |
| VOL. 26 – ELVIS PRESLEY | 00699643 / $16.99 |
| VOL. 27 – DAVID LEE ROTH | 00699645 / $16.95 |
| VOL. 28 – GREG KOCH | 00699646 / $16.99 |
| VOL. 29 – BOB SEGER | 00699647 / $15.99 |
| VOL. 30 – KISS | 00699644 / $16.99 |
| VOL. 32 – THE OFFSPRING | 00699653 / $14.95 |
| VOL. 33 – ACOUSTIC CLASSICS | 00699656 / $17.99 |
| VOL. 34 – CLASSIC ROCK | 00699658 / $17.99 |
| VOL. 35 – HAIR METAL | 00699660 / $17.99 |
| VOL. 36 – SOUTHERN ROCK | 00699661 / $17.99 |
| VOL. 37 – ACOUSTIC UNPLUGGED | 00699662 / $22.99 |
| VOL. 38 – BLUES | 00699663 / $16.95 |
| VOL. 39 – '80S METAL | 00699664 / $16.99 |
| VOL. 40 – INCUBUS | 00699668 / $17.95 |
| VOL. 41 – ERIC CLAPTON | 00699669 / $17.99 |
| VOL. 42 – COVER BAND HITS | 00211597 / $16.99 |
| VOL. 43 – LYNYRD SKYNYRD | 00699681 / $17.95 |
| VOL. 44 – JAZZ | 00699689 / $16.99 |
| VOL. 45 – TV THEMES | 00699718 / $14.95 |
| VOL. 46 – MAINSTREAM ROCK | 00699722 / $16.95 |
| VOL. 47 – HENDRIX SMASH HITS | 00699723 / $19.99 |
| VOL. 48 – AEROSMITH CLASSICS | 00699724 / $17.99 |
| VOL. 49 – STEVIE RAY VAUGHAN | 00699725 / $17.99 |
| VOL. 50 – VAN HALEN 1978-1984 | 00110269 / $17.99 |
| VOL. 51 – ALTERNATIVE '90S | 00699727 / $14.99 |
| VOL. 52 – FUNK | 00699728 / $15.99 |
| VOL. 53 – DISCO | 00699729 / $14.99 |
| VOL. 54 – HEAVY METAL | 00699730 / $15.99 |
| VOL. 55 – POP METAL | 00699731 / $14.95 |
| VOL. 56 – FOO FIGHTERS | 00699749 / $15.99 |
| VOL. 59 – CHET ATKINS | 00702347 / $16.99 |
| VOL. 62 – CHRISTMAS CAROLS | 00699798 / $12.95 |
| VOL. 63 – CREEDENCE CLEARWATER REVIVAL | 00699802 / $16.99 |
| VOL. 64 – THE ULTIMATE OZZY OSBOURNE | 00699803 / $17.99 |
| VOL. 66 – THE ROLLING STONES | 00699807 / $17.99 |
| VOL. 67 – BLACK SABBATH | 00699808 / $16.99 |
| VOL. 68 – PINK FLOYD – DARK SIDE OF THE MOON | 00699809 / $16.99 |

| | |
|---|---|
| VOL. 69 – ACOUSTIC FAVORITES | 00699810 / $16.99 |
| VOL. 70 – OZZY OSBOURNE | 00699805 / $16.99 |
| VOL. 73 – BLUESY ROCK | 00699829 / $16.99 |
| VOL. 74 – SIMPLE STRUMMING SONGS | 00151706 / $19.99 |
| VOL. 75 – TOM PETTY | 00699882 / $16.99 |
| VOL. 76 – COUNTRY HITS | 00699884 / $16.99 |
| VOL. 77 – BLUEGRASS | 00699910 / $15.99 |
| VOL. 78 – NIRVANA | 00700132 / $16.99 |
| VOL. 79 – NEIL YOUNG | 00700133 / $24.99 |
| VOL. 80 – ACOUSTIC ANTHOLOGY | 00700175 / $19.95 |
| VOL. 81 – ROCK ANTHOLOGY | 00700176 / $22.99 |
| VOL. 82 – EASY SONGS | 00700177 / $14.99 |
| VOL. 83 – THREE CHORD SONGS | 00700178 / $16.99 |
| VOL. 84 – STEELY DAN | 00700200 / $16.99 |
| VOL. 85 – THE POLICE | 00700269 / $16.99 |
| VOL. 86 – BOSTON | 00700465 / $16.99 |
| VOL. 87 – ACOUSTIC WOMEN | 00700763 / $14.99 |
| VOL. 89 – REGGAE | 00700468 / $15.99 |
| VOL. 90 – CLASSICAL POP | 00700469 / $14.99 |
| VOL. 91 – BLUES INSTRUMENTALS | 00700505 / $15.99 |
| VOL. 92 – EARLY ROCK INSTRUMENTALS | 00700506 / $15.99 |
| VOL. 93 – ROCK INSTRUMENTALS | 00700507 / $16.99 |
| VOL. 94 – SLOW BLUES | 00700508 / $16.99 |
| VOL. 95 – BLUES CLASSICS | 00700509 / $15.99 |
| VOL. 96 – BEST COUNTRY HITS | 00211615 / $16.99 |
| VOL. 97 – CHRISTMAS CLASSICS | 00236542 / $14.99 |
| VOL. 99 – ZZ TOP | 00700762 / $16.99 |
| VOL. 100 – B.B. KING | 00700466 / $16.99 |
| VOL. 101 – SONGS FOR BEGINNERS | 00701917 / $14.99 |
| VOL. 102 – CLASSIC PUNK | 00700769 / $14.99 |
| VOL. 103 – SWITCHFOOT | 00700773 / $16.99 |
| VOL. 104 – DUANE ALLMAN | 00700846 / $16.99 |
| VOL. 105 – LATIN | 00700939 / $16.99 |
| VOL. 106 – WEEZER | 00700958 / $14.99 |
| VOL. 107 – CREAM | 00701069 / $16.99 |
| VOL. 108 – THE WHO | 00701053 / $16.99 |
| VOL. 109 – STEVE MILLER | 00701054 / $17.99 |
| VOL. 110 – SLIDE GUITAR HITS | 00701055 / $16.99 |
| VOL. 111 – JOHN MELLENCAMP | 00701056 / $14.99 |
| VOL. 112 – QUEEN | 00701052 / $16.99 |
| VOL. 113 – JIM CROCE | 00701058 / $16.99 |
| VOL. 114 – BON JOVI | 00701060 / $16.99 |
| VOL. 115 – JOHNNY CASH | 00701070 / $16.99 |
| VOL. 116 – THE VENTURES | 00701124 / $16.99 |
| VOL. 117 – BRAD PAISLEY | 00701224 / $16.99 |
| VOL. 118 – ERIC JOHNSON | 00701353 / $16.99 |
| VOL. 119 – AC/DC CLASSICS | 00701356 / $17.99 |
| VOL. 120 – PROGRESSIVE ROCK | 00701457 / $14.99 |
| VOL. 121 – U2 | 00701508 / $16.99 |
| VOL. 122 – CROSBY, STILLS & NASH | 00701610 / $16.99 |
| VOL. 123 – LENNON & MCCARTNEY ACOUSTIC | 00701614 / $16.99 |
| VOL. 125 – JEFF BECK | 00701687 / $16.99 |
| VOL. 126 – BOB MARLEY | 00701701 / $16.99 |
| VOL. 127 – 1970S ROCK | 00701739 / $16.99 |
| VOL. 128 – 1960S ROCK | 00701740 / $14.99 |
| VOL. 129 – MEGADETH | 00701741 / $16.99 |
| VOL. 130 – IRON MAIDEN | 00701742 / $17.99 |
| VOL. 131 – 1990S ROCK | 00701743 / $14.99 |
| VOL. 132 – COUNTRY ROCK | 00701757 / $15.99 |
| VOL. 133 – TAYLOR SWIFT | 00701894 / $16.99 |
| VOL. 134 – AVENGED SEVENFOLD | 00701906 / $16.99 |
| VOL. 135 – MINOR BLUES | 00151350 / $17.99 |
| VOL. 136 – GUITAR THEMES | 00701922 / $14.99 |

| | |
|---|---|
| VOL. 137 – IRISH TUNES | 00701966 / $15.99 |
| VOL. 138 – BLUEGRASS CLASSICS | 00701967 / $16.99 |
| VOL. 139 – GARY MOORE | 00702370 / $16.99 |
| VOL. 140 – MORE STEVIE RAY VAUGHAN | 00702396 / $17.99 |
| VOL. 141 – ACOUSTIC HITS | 00702401 / $16.99 |
| VOL. 142 – GEORGE HARRISON | 00237697 / $17.99 |
| VOL. 143 – SLASH | 00702425 / $19.99 |
| VOL. 144 – DJANGO REINHARDT | 00702531 / $16.99 |
| VOL. 145 – DEF LEPPARD | 00702532 / $17.99 |
| VOL. 146 – ROBERT JOHNSON | 00702533 / $16.99 |
| VOL. 147 – SIMON & GARFUNKEL | 14041591 / $16.99 |
| VOL. 148 – BOB DYLAN | 14041592 / $16.99 |
| VOL. 149 – AC/DC HITS | 14041593 / $17.99 |
| VOL. 150 – ZAKK WYLDE | 02501717 / $16.99 |
| VOL. 151 – J.S. BACH | 02501730 / $16.99 |
| VOL. 152 – JOE BONAMASSA | 02501751 / $19.99 |
| VOL. 153 – RED HOT CHILI PEPPERS | 00702990 / $19.99 |
| VOL. 155 – ERIC CLAPTON – FROM THE ALBUM UNPLUGGED | 00703085 / $16.99 |
| VOL. 156 – SLAYER | 00703770 / $17.99 |
| VOL. 157 – FLEETWOOD MAC | 00101382 / $16.99 |
| VOL. 159 – WES MONTGOMERY | 00102593 / $19.99 |
| VOL. 160 – T-BONE WALKER | 00102641 / $16.99 |
| VOL. 161 – THE EAGLES – ACOUSTIC | 00102659 / $17.99 |
| VOL. 162 – THE EAGLES HITS | 00102667 / $17.99 |
| VOL. 163 – PANTERA | 00103036 / $17.99 |
| VOL. 164 – VAN HALEN 1986-1995 | 00110270 / $17.99 |
| VOL. 165 – GREEN DAY | 00210343 / $17.99 |
| VOL. 166 – MODERN BLUES | 00700764 / $16.99 |
| VOL. 167 – DREAM THEATER | 00111938 / $24.99 |
| VOL. 168 – KISS | 00113421 / $16.99 |
| VOL. 169 – TAYLOR SWIFT | 00115982 / $16.99 |
| VOL. 170 – THREE DAYS GRACE | 00117337 / $16.99 |
| VOL. 171 – JAMES BROWN | 00117420 / $16.99 |
| VOL. 172 – THE DOOBIE BROTHERS | 00119670 / $16.99 |
| VOL. 173 – TRANS-SIBERIAN ORCHESTRA | 00119907 / $19.99 |
| VOL. 174 – SCORPIONS | 00122119 / $16.99 |
| VOL. 175 – MICHAEL SCHENKER | 00122127 / $16.99 |
| VOL. 176 – BLUES BREAKERS WITH JOHN MAYALL & ERIC CLAPTON | 00122132 / $19.99 |
| VOL. 177 – ALBERT KING | 00123271 / $16.99 |
| VOL. 178 – JASON MRAZ | 00124165 / $17.99 |
| VOL. 179 – RAMONES | 00127073 / $16.99 |
| VOL. 180 – BRUNO MARS | 00129706 / $16.99 |
| VOL. 181 – JACK JOHNSON | 00129854 / $16.99 |
| VOL. 182 – SOUNDGARDEN | 00138161 / $17.99 |
| VOL. 183 – BUDDY GUY | 00138240 / $17.99 |
| VOL. 184 – KENNY WAYNE SHEPHERD | 00138258 / $17.99 |
| VOL. 185 – JOE SATRIANI | 00139457 / $17.99 |
| VOL. 186 – GRATEFUL DEAD | 00139459 / $17.99 |
| VOL. 187 – JOHN DENVER | 00140839 / $17.99 |
| VOL. 188 – MÖTLEY CRUE | 00141145 / $17.99 |
| VOL. 189 – JOHN MAYER | 00144350 / $17.99 |
| VOL. 191 – PINK FLOYD CLASSICS | 00146164 / $17.99 |
| VOL. 192 – JUDAS PRIEST | 00151352 / $17.99 |
| VOL. 195 – METALLICA: 1983-1988 | 00234291 / $19.99 |

*Prices, contents, and availability subject to change without notice.*

**Complete song lists available online.**

HAL•LEONARD®
www.halleonard.com

0618

# RECORDED VERSIONS®

## The Best Note-For-Note Transcriptions Available

**AUTHENTIC TRANSCRIPTIONS WITH NOTES AND TABLATURE**

| | | |
|---|---|---|
| 14037551 | AC/DC – Backtracks | $32.99 |
| 00690178 | Alice in Chains – Acoustic | $19.99 |
| 00694865 | Alice in Chains – Dirt | $19.99 |
| 00690958 | Duane Allman Guitar Anthology | $24.99 |
| 00694932 | Allman Brothers Band – Volume 1 | $24.95 |
| 00694933 | Allman Brothers Band – Volume 2 | $24.95 |
| 00694934 | Allman Brothers Band – Volume 3 | $24.99 |
| 00123558 | Arctic Monkeys – AM | $22.99 |
| 00690609 | Audioslave | $19.95 |
| 00690820 | Avenged Sevenfold – City of Evil | $24.95 |
| 00691065 | Avenged Sevenfold – Waking the Fallen | $22.99 |
| 00123140 | The Avett Brothers Guitar Collection | $22.99 |
| 00690503 | Beach Boys – Very Best of | $19.99 |
| 00690489 | Beatles – 1 | $24.99 |
| 00694832 | Beatles – For Acoustic Guitar | $24.99 |
| 00691014 | Beatles Rock Band | $34.99 |
| 00694914 | Beatles – Rubber Soul | $22.99 |
| 00694863 | Beatles – Sgt. Pepper's Lonely Hearts Club Band | $22.99 |
| 00110193 | Beatles – Tomorrow Never Knows | $22.99 |
| 00690110 | Beatles – White Album (Book 1) | $19.99 |
| 00691043 | Jeff Beck – Wired | $19.99 |
| 00692385 | Chuck Berry | $22.99 |
| 00690835 | Billy Talent | $19.95 |
| 00147787 | Best of the Black Crowes | $19.99 |
| 00690901 | Best of Black Sabbath | $19.95 |
| 14042759 | Black Sabbath – 13 | $19.99 |
| 00690831 | blink-182 – Greatest Hits | $19.95 |
| 00148544 | Michael Bloomfield Guitar Anthology | $24.99 |
| 00158600 | Joe Bonamassa – Blues of Desperation | $22.99 |
| 00160988 | Bootleg Country Guitar Tabs | $19.99 |
| 00690913 | Boston | $19.95 |
| 00690491 | David Bowie – Best of | $19.99 |
| 00690873 | Breaking Benjamin – Phobia | $19.95 |
| 00141446 | Best of Lenny Breau | $19.99 |
| 00690451 | Jeff Buckley – Collection | $24.95 |
| 00690957 | Bullet for My Valentine – Scream Aim Fire | $22.99 |
| 00691159 | The Cars – Complete Greatest Hits | $22.99 |
| 00691079 | Best of Johnny Cash | $22.99 |
| 00690590 | Eric Clapton – Anthology | $29.95 |
| 00690415 | Clapton Chronicles – Best of Eric Clapton | $18.95 |
| 00690936 | Eric Clapton – Complete Clapton | $29.99 |
| 00192383 | Eric Clapton – I Still Do* | $19.99 |
| 00694869 | Eric Clapton – Unplugged | $22.95 |
| 00138731 | Eric Clapton & Friends – The Breeze | $22.99 |
| 00690162 | The Clash – Best of | $19.95 |
| 00101916 | Eric Church – Chief | $22.99 |
| 00690828 | Coheed & Cambria – Good Apollo I'm Burning Star, IV, Vol. 1: From Fear Through the Eyes of Madness | $19.95 |
| 00141704 | Jesse Cook – Works Vol. 1 | $19.99 |
| 00127184 | Best of Robert Cray | $19.99 |
| 00690819 | Creedence Clearwater Revival – Best of | $24.99 |
| 00690648 | The Very Best of Jim Croce | $19.99 |
| 00690613 | Crosby, Stills & Nash – Best of | $22.95 |
| 00691171 | Cry of Love – Brother | $22.99 |
| 00690967 | Death Cab for Cutie – Narrow Stairs | $22.99 |
| 00690289 | Deep Purple – Best of | $19.99 |
| 00690784 | Def Leppard – Best of | $22.99 |
| 00692240 | Bo Diddley | $19.99 |
| 00122443 | Dream Theater | $24.99 |
| 14041903 | Bob Dylan for Guitar Tab | $19.99 |
| 00172824 | Tommy Emmanuel – It's Never Too Late | $22.99 |
| 00139220 | Tommy Emmanuel – Little by Little | $24.99 |
| 00691186 | Evanescence | $22.99 |
| 00691181 | Five Finger Death Punch – American Capitalist | $22.99 |
| 00690664 | Fleetwood Mac – Best of | $22.99 |
| 00691115 | Foo Fighters – Wasting Light | $22.99 |
| 00690805 | Robben Ford – Best of | $22.99 |
| 00120220 | Robben Ford – Guitar Anthology | $24.99 |

| | | |
|---|---|---|
| 00694920 | Free – Best of | $19.99 |
| 00691190 | Best of Peter Green | $19.99 |
| 00212480 | Green Day – Revolutionary Radio* | $19.99 |
| 00690840 | Ben Harper – Both Sides of the Gun | $19.95 |
| 00694798 | George Harrison – Anthology | $19.95 |
| 00690841 | Scott Henderson – Blues Guitar Collection | $22.99 |
| 00692930 | Jimi Hendrix – Are You Experienced? | $24.95 |
| 00692931 | Jimi Hendrix – Axis: Bold As Love | $22.95 |
| 00275044 | Jimi Hendrix – Both Sides of the Sky | $22.99 |
| 00692932 | Jimi Hendrix – Electric Ladyland | $24.95 |
| 00690017 | Jimi Hendrix – Live at Woodstock | $27.50 |
| 00690602 | Jimi Hendrix – Smash Hits | $24.99 |
| 00119619 | Jimi Hendrix – People, Hell and Angels | $22.99 |
| 00691152 | West Coast Seattle Boy: The Jimi Hendrix Anthology | $29.99 |
| 00691332 | Jimi Hendrix – Winterland (Highlights) | $22.99 |
| 00690793 | John Lee Hooker Anthology | $24.99 |
| 00121961 | Imagine Dragons – Night Visions | $22.99 |
| 00690688 | Incubus – A Crow Left of the Murder | $19.95 |
| 00690790 | Iron Maiden Anthology | $24.99 |
| 00690684 | Jethro Tull – Aqualung | $19.99 |
| 00690751 | John5 – Vertigo | $19.95 |
| 00122439 | Jack Johnson – From Here to Now to You | $22.99 |
| 00690271 | Robert Johnson – New Transcriptions | $24.99 |
| 00699131 | Janis Joplin – Best of | $19.95 |
| 00690427 | Judas Priest – Best of | $24.99 |
| 00120814 | Killswitch Engage – Disarm the Descent | $22.99 |
| 00124869 | Albert King with Stevie Ray Vaughan – In Session | $22.99 |
| 00694903 | Kiss – Best of | $24.99 |
| 00690355 | Kiss – Destroyer | $16.95 |
| 00690834 | Lamb of God – Ashes of the Wake | $19.95 |
| 00690875 | Lamb of God – Sacrament | $19.95 |
| 00114563 | The Lumineers | $22.99 |
| 00690955 | Lynyrd Skynyrd – All-Time Greatest Hits | $22.99 |
| 00694954 | Lynyrd Skynyrd – New Best of | $22.99 |
| 00209846 | Mammoth Metal Guitar Tab Anthology | $29.99 |
| 00690754 | Marilyn Manson – Lest We Forget | $19.99 |
| 00694956 | Bob Marley – Legend | $19.95 |
| 00694945 | Bob Marley – Songs of Freedom | $24.95 |
| 00139168 | Pat Martino – Guitar Anthology | $24.99 |
| 00129105 | John McLaughlin Guitar Tab Anthology | $24.99 |
| 00120080 | Don McLean – Songbook | $19.99 |
| 00694951 | Megadeth – Rust in Peace | $24.99 |
| 00691185 | Megadeth – Th1rt3en | $22.99 |
| 00690505 | John Mellencamp – Guitar Collection | $19.99 |
| 00209876 | Metallica – Hardwired...To Self-Destruct | $22.99 |
| 00690646 | Pat Metheny – One Quiet Night | $19.95 |
| 00690558 | Pat Metheny – Trio: 99>00 | $24.99 |
| 00118836 | Pat Metheny – Unity Band | $22.99 |
| 00690040 | Steve Miller Band – Young Hearts | $19.99 |
| 00119338 | Ministry Guitar Tab Collection | $24.99 |
| 00102591 | Wes Montgomery Guitar Anthology | $24.99 |
| 00691070 | Mumford & Sons – Sigh No More | $22.99 |
| 00151195 | Muse – Drones | $19.99 |
| 00694883 | Nirvana – Nevermind | $19.95 |
| 00690026 | Nirvana – Unplugged in New York | $19.95 |
| 00243349 | The Best of Opeth | $22.99 |
| 00694847 | Ozzy Osbourne – Best of | $24.99 |
| 00690933 | Best of Brad Paisley | $24.99 |
| 00690995 | Brad Paisley – Play: The Guitar Album | $24.99 |
| 00694855 | Pearl Jam – Ten | $22.99 |
| 00690439 | A Perfect Circle – Mer De Noms | $19.95 |
| 00690499 | Tom Petty – Definitive Guitar Collection | $19.99 |
| 00121933 | Pink Floyd – Acoustic Guitar Collection | $24.99 |
| 00690428 | Pink Floyd – Dark Side of the Moon | $19.95 |
| 00239799 | Pink Floyd – The Wall | $24.99 |
| 00690789 | Poison – Best of | $19.99 |
| 00694975 | Queen – Greatest Hits | $24.95 |
| 00254332 | Queens of the Stone Age – Villains | $22.99 |
| 00690670 | Queensryche – Very Best of | $24.99 |
| 00109303 | Radiohead Guitar Anthology | $24.99 |
| 00694910 | Rage Against the Machine | $19.95 |
| 00119834 | Rage Against the Machine – Guitar Anthology | $22.99 |

| | | |
|---|---|---|
| 00690055 | Red Hot Chili Peppers – Blood Sugar Sex Magik | $19.95 |
| 00690584 | Red Hot Chili Peppers – By the Way | $19.95 |
| 00691166 | Red Hot Chili Peppers – I'm with You | $22.99 |
| 00690852 | Red Hot Chili Peppers –Stadium Arcadium | $24.95 |
| 00690511 | Django Reinhardt – Definitive Collection | $22.99 |
| 14043417 | Rodrigo y Gabriela – 9 Dead Alive | $19.99 |
| 00690631 | Rolling Stones – Guitar Anthology | $27.95 |
| 00694976 | Rolling Stones – Some Girls | $22.95 |
| 00690264 | The Rolling Stones – Tattoo You | $19.95 |
| 00690685 | David Lee Roth – Eat 'Em and Smile | $22.99 |
| 00690942 | David Lee Roth and the Songs of Van Halen | $19.95 |
| 00151826 | Royal Blood | $22.99 |
| 00690031 | Santana's Greatest Hits | $19.95 |
| 00276350 | Joe Satriani – What Happens Next | $24.99 |
| 00128870 | Matt Schofield Guitar Tab Collection | $22.99 |
| 00690566 | Scorpions – Best of | $24.99 |
| 00690604 | Bob Seger – Guitar Collection | $22.99 |
| 00234543 | Ed Sheeran – Divide | $19.99 |
| 00138870 | Ed Sheeran – X | $19.99 |
| 00690803 | Kenny Wayne Shepherd Band – Best of | $19.95 |
| 00151178 | Kenny Wayne Shepherd – Ledbetter Heights (20th Anniversary Edition) | $19.99 |
| 00122218 | Skillet – Rise | $22.99 |
| 00691114 | Slash – Guitar Anthology | $24.99 |
| 00690813 | Slayer – Guitar Collection | $19.99 |
| 00120004 | Steely Dan – Best of | $24.95 |
| 00694921 | Steppenwolf – Best of | $22.95 |
| 00690655 | Mike Stern – Best of | $24.99 |
| 00690520 | Styx Guitar Collection | $19.95 |
| 00120081 | Sublime | $19.99 |
| 00120122 | Sublime – 40oz. to Freedom | $19.95 |
| 00690767 | Switchfoot – The Beautiful Letdown | $19.95 |
| 00690993 | Taylor Swift – Fearless | $22.99 |
| 00115957 | Taylor Swift – Red | $21.99 |
| 00690531 | System of a Down – Toxicity | $19.95 |
| 00694824 | James Taylor – Best of | $19.99 |
| 00150209 | Trans-Siberian Orchestra Guitar Anthology | $19.99 |
| 00253237 | Trivium – Guitar Tab Anthology | $24.99 |
| 00123862 | Trivium – Vengeance Falls | $22.99 |
| 00690683 | Robin Trower – Bridge of Sighs | $19.95 |
| 00660137 | Steve Vai – Passion & Warfare | $24.95 |
| 00110385 | Steve Vai – The Story of Light | $22.99 |
| 00690116 | Stevie Ray Vaughan – Guitar Collection | $24.95 |
| 00660058 | Stevie Ray Vaughan – Lightnin' Blues 1983-1987 | $27.99 |
| 00217455 | Stevie Ray Vaughan – Plays Slow Blues | $19.99 |
| 00694835 | Stevie Ray Vaughan – The Sky Is Crying | $22.95 |
| 00690015 | Stevie Ray Vaughan – Texas Flood | $19.99 |
| 00183213 | Volbeat – Seal the Deal & Let's Boogie* | $19.99 |
| 00152161 | Doc Watson – Guitar Anthology | $22.99 |
| 00690071 | Weezer (The Blue Album) | $19.95 |
| 00172118 | Weezer – (The White Album)* | $19.99 |
| 00691941 | The Who – Acoustic Guitar Collection | $22.99 |
| 00690447 | The Who – Best of | $24.95 |
| 00122303 | Yes Guitar Collection | $22.99 |
| 00690916 | The Best of Dwight Yoakam | $19.95 |
| 00691020 | Neil Young – After the Gold Rush | $22.99 |
| 00691019 | Neil Young – Everybody Knows This Is Nowhere | $19.99 |
| 00691021 | Neil Young – Harvest Moon | $22.99 |
| 00690905 | Neil Young – Rust Never Sleeps | $19.99 |
| 00690623 | Frank Zappa – Over-Nite Sensation | $22.99 |
| 00121684 | ZZ Top – Early Classics | $24.99 |
| 00690589 | ZZ Top Guitar Anthology | $24.99 |

**COMPLETE SERIES LIST ONLINE!**

**HAL•LEONARD®**
www.halleonard.com

Prices and availability subject to change without notice.
*Tab transcriptions only.